# A.G.I.L.E. Thinking Demystified

# A.G.I.L.E. Thinking Demystified

## Mindset Over Mechanics

Frank M. Forte

**BEP**
BUSINESS EXPERT PRESS
Leader in applied, concise business books

First published in 2021 by
Business Expert Press, LLC
222 East 46th Street, New York, NY 10017
www.businessexpertpress.com

ISBN-13: 978-1-63157-903-5 (paperback)
ISBN-13: 978-1-63157-904-2 (e-book)

Business Expert Press Portfolio and Project Management Collection

Collection ISSN: 2156-8189 (print)
Collection ISSN: 2156-8200 (electronic)

Cover image licensed by Ingram Image, StockPhotoSecrets.com
Cover and interior design by S4Carlisle Publishing Services Private Ltd., Chennai, India

First edition: 2021

10 9 8 7 6 5 4 3 2 1

Printed in the United States of America.

# Dedication

*To my wife, Christine, of 41 years of marriage, and my three sons, Joseph, Carl, and James, currently serving in the U.S. Army. To their three wives, Stephanie, Amy, and Mandy. Last, and certainly not least, to my seven wonderful grandchildren, Arianna, Kenzie, Alexander, Lucas, Sadie, Penelope, and Gregory. You give me hope, joy, and purpose.*

*Love, Frank, Dad, Grandpa*

# Acknowledgment

Thanks to all of those who have supported my agile journey. I want to especially thank all of those that have contributed to this book through many conversations, some late into the evening. Finally, I would like to thank Tim Kloppenborg for seeing a book in me before I did.

# Abstract

Agile has proven to be the go-to approach to begin to transform organizations in the digital age. Without agile, large organizations struggle to keep up with their nimbler competitors. There are not only external threats, but also internal threats. Employees want to work for customer obsessed organizations that have more than just a profit motive. Agile goes a long way in convincing existing and potential talent that you are the right place for them. Customers have many more options today than they did in the last century, so agile is a way to rally your entire organization toward becoming customer obsessed. All of the potential benefits of agile will not be realized until the leaders first have a higher-level understanding of the mindset that is critical to undertaking the successful journey to becoming more agile.

This book provides readers with an understanding of how to take full advantage of agility at the enterprise level, including deep work required on the following fronts:

- The organization expanding their thinking and behavior.
- The organization creating new processes to support the use of agile.
- Individuals growing in the use of empiricism, which is the foundation of agility.
- Leaders taking on new roles and focusing on different activities.

The framework of this book will help develop a new way of thinking and is anchored in

- **A**daptability
- **G**rowth
- **I**mprovement
- **L**eadership
- **E**xperience

In order to make the full transition to thinking in an A.G.I.L.E. way, you will need to challenge everything you think you know about leading and working in large organizations. That is the purpose of this book.

# Keywords

agile, mindset, plan-driven, transformation, change, empiricism, failure, leadership, learning

# Contents

# Preface

There is a new movement forming within society that encourages organizations to work in different ways than we have been working since the beginning of the industrial age. We are seeking to have people bring their creative and entrepreneurial ideas to work instead of simply delivering on tasks that are organized and managed by others. In reality, this movement is causing us to treat people as something other than things that produce other things. This requires us to lead instead of manage, as I ascribe to the belief that we manage things and lead people.

This change is a challenge for large organizations who have been thinking and working in a certain way for decades. Many of the people within the highest levels of these organizations have been very successful by thinking in a particular way about work and the people who do that work. In many cases, these thoughts are built around a plan-driven approach to getting things done. While this approach is useful in many repeatable applications where things are done exactly the same way and by the same people, it is less so when it comes to work that we have not done before. When we have multiple variables, we cannot expect predictable, controlled outputs as many leaders expect. So, those same leaders look for the variables in the equation, which quickly leads to the people. Most people want to do a good job, work hard, and contribute. So why the disconnect between expectations and outputs?

As we learn about the nature of work in the digital age, we begin to see complexity and uncertainty around every turn, which can often bring us to the point where we are on the verge of chaos. This is when leaders with experience in a command and control model excel and where someone in control is needed to decide where they will go and what they will do as an organization next. While this heavy hand is needed when in chaos, a system cannot be in chaos often, or else it is not a system. As soon as we begin to walk back from chaos, we need to give control back to the people doing the work and allow them to create in a way that is sustainable for them to do so.

In this book, there will be apparent contradictions, as this is a complex transition that we as leaders will experience. We must understand that we need to think in a different way if we hope to make the changes needed. To have a chance at making a real change in industries and organizations, we need to deeply experience how to think in a different way as we move through our environment going forward. Not all of the answers are laid out in this book and there is much more to understand about how we can become more agile as organizations. The following is a list of other books in this series that compliment and support this book. It is strongly recommended that you explore these titles as this work is an advanced presentation of the mindset needed to make agile work at scale.

1. Paquette, Paul, and Milan Frankl. *Agile Project Management for Business Transformation Success*. New York, NY: Business Expert Press, 2016.
2. Vanderjack, Brian. *The Agile Edge: Managing Projects Effectively Using Agile Scrum*. New York, NY: Business Expert Press, 2015.
3. Hoogveld, Mike. Agile Management: *The Fast and Flexible Approach to Continuous Improvement and Innovation in Organizations*. New York, NY: Business Expert Press, 2018.
4. Nicolaas, Dion. *Scrum for Teams: A Guide by Practical Example*. New York, NY: Business Expert Press, 2018.
5. Eary, John. *Agile Working and the Digital Workspace: Best Practices for Designing and Implementing Productivity*. New York, NY: Business Expert Press, 2018.

As we seek to understand how to move to a more A.G.I.L.E way of being, we often examine new companies that have been built from the ground up to perform in a more A.G.I.L.E way. Unfortunately, that approach does not work when we are moving well established organizations to a more A.G.I.L.E way of thinking. We also cannot use traditional change management approaches, which are primarily based on plan-driven change models that presuppose a result or outcome that is known.

So, where does the insight for helping navigate large, well-established organizations to thinking in a more A.G.I.L.E way originate? This is the fundamental question explored in this book.

# Author's Note

It would be great for everyone that is interested in agile to read this book, however it is not for the beginner. There are books in this series that will give you a good foundation. It also takes experience to understand what is being discussed in these pages. Here is my advice:

Take your time and reflect on the sections. Come back to them periodically. Pick up the book and find something of interest. Do not think that you will be able to read this straight through once and get everything you can from it. You will change as you grow in thinking in an A.G.I.L.E way. Be patient with yourself and with your organization.

There are two uses of the word agile in this book;

1. agile is used to describe the general use of the word
2. A.G.I.L.E is used to identify the new way of thinking described throughout this book.

# Introduction

The word agile has become synonymous with change in technology organizations both large and small; however, there is an emerging misconception of how agile can be used to make a significant change in complex endeavors. Creating an acronym from the word agile teaches leaders and workers alike how to work with this new way of thinking.

**A**daptability
**G**rowth
**I**mprovement
**L**eadership
**E**xperience

The author explores how all organizations can embrace a way of thinking that will allow the benefits of agile to be realized. Most of the books on this subject focus on identifying the mechanics of a particular practice within the agile space but fail to define the overarching thinking that makes them so effective. These include, but are not limited to, the use of Scrum, XP, or Kanban. While these are necessary works and lay the foundation for agile practices, they do not address the mindset shift to take full advantage of these practices. They also lack advice on how to use these practices in a determined and purposeful way to continue to grow in an agile way of thinking.

# PART 1

# Laying the Foundation

<table>
<tr><td>Adaptability</td></tr>
<tr><td>Growth</td></tr>
<tr><td>Improvement</td></tr>
<tr><td>Leadership</td></tr>
<tr><td>Experience</td></tr>
</table>

## Adaptability

**Objectives:**

1. Recognize individuals must show up differently.
2. Understand how to leverage customer feedback.
3. Realize customers are less concerned about adherence to a plan than the correct outcomes.

Adaptability is of paramount importance to thinking in an A.G.I.L.E. way. The pace of change within organizations, for whatever reason, is increasing, and that increase demands that we adapt to be successful. In order to benefit from the effort of going agile, individuals must show up differently. The common challenges we face at the individual level that must be addressed in the bottom-up approach are these behavioral changes. Individuals must become aware of the changes in themselves in order to receive the benefit of working agile. They become able to see the lack of that same behavior in other team members, resulting in a rich environment for experiential learning.

When we have momentum through the acceleration of embracing the A.G.I.L.E way of thinking, we will be able to pivot quickly when we get feedback on our product. The need for feedback is one of the many challenges that the plan-driven approach has been unable to support. This has created a disconnect between the customer and the producer of the product. Since we are normally developing products that require many people to produce, we do not know if we are delivering on the outcomes the customer seeks without proper feedback. If we have a customer and a stated desire, we need to get a working product in their hand. We use different approaches to do this quickly; however, the longer it takes to deliver the output to the customer, the further away we are from realizing the full potential of this way of thinking. In many cases, it will take years for large organizations to remove the impediments that the plan-driven approach has instituted to ensure predictability against a documented plan versus the product outcomes customers seek.

The organization is not the driver of A.G.I.L.E. thinking; it is the recipient. In agile, it is the individuals within the organization who help move it in a direction that allows agile to grow and thrive. We must, however, monitor the system to ensure we are seeing indications, both good and bad, of the effects A.G.I.L.E. thinking is having on the organization.

The organizational level may be the hardest level to break through and, depending on the product being produced, may come sooner or later compared with other areas of adaptability. A.G.I.L.E. thinking shows up in results for the customer, which may take some time as we have had to significantly impact the organization along the way to get to where the customer will see the benefits of working in an A. G. I. L. E. manner. How do we tell whether our customers will even value agile as we do as an organization? The value will be determined by the market response to whatever outcomes we seek by endeavoring to think in a more A.G.I.L.E. way.

The individual must become part of a team that is focused on the same goal for short periods of time. Two weeks is normally long enough to get a finished product out without allowing too much time for the student syndrome to take over or for the work to expand beyond what is absolutely necessary for a working product. The student syndrome is when students think they have until the end of the grading period to turn in a paper, so they do not start on it soon enough, which often results in the paper lacking the quality they hoped for at the beginning of the grading period. This same behavior is seen with teams beginning to work in an A.G.I.L.E. way. To help guard against this, a shorter period is used to ensure there is a sense of urgency.

As individuals begin to adapt to this new way of working, they will notice changes in their own ways of working and will be able to either quickly embrace or resist this A.G.I.L.E. approach for any of several reasons:

- A lack of autonomy (they are now part of a team)
- Increased transparency (everyone on the team can see what they are doing)
- A lack of alignment with the team goals personally

As individuals become aware of the changes in themselves, they will need to work on coming into better alignment with the A.G.I.L.E. way of thinking and their team members in order to receive the benefits. Individuals will become aware of this resistance in others, as well. The team will need to address this resistance in order to move to higher levels of performance. This awareness will present a rich environment for experiential learning; however, this will not happen quickly, and those that want to embrace A.G.I.L.E. thinking will need to bear in mind that it will take time. It is critical that time is given to stable groups of individuals so they can begin to work together toward A.G.I.L.E. thinking.

As we continue to adapt to the A.G.I.L.E. approach, we eventually come to the place where we have larger and larger groups of people who are working and thinking in a more A.G.I.L.E. way. This will create opportunities for the organization to look at their systems and see what is impeding this new way of thinking and what is working.

If an organization has been optimized to work in a plan-driven approach, it is reasonable to expect that the systems they have in place have been optimized for this purpose. Even if not formally done, individuals have been taught or have learned through observation to conform to *the way we have always done things*. With A.G.I.L.E., we are asking them to begin working and thinking differently. This challenge at the organizational level will become even more difficult when we realize that most large organizations will have the traditional plan-driven approach in place while the A.G.I.L.E. way of thinking is experimented with and determinations are made as to where best to apply this way of thinking.

**Reflection:**

1. What can organizations do to encourage the absorption of agile?
2. What can individuals do to embrace the A.G.I.L.E. way of thinking?
3. What are some of the options open to individuals and organizations when there is a fundamental mismatch with the A.G.I.L.E. way of thinking?

Adaptability

Growth

Improvement

Leadership

Experience

# Growth

**Objectives:**
1. Demonstrate the need for growth.
2. Recognize the ways that A.G.I.L.E. thinking allows for growth.
3. Become comfortable with being uncomfortable in this new environment.

If we are not growing, we are dying. How do we ensure our organization is growing the right way for the work we do and the people with whom we do that work? Are we growing at a pace that gives our stakeholders confidence and builds trust, or are we discouraging our stakeholders from trusting us to be ready no matter what the future brings?

A.G.I.L.E. thinking exposes opportunities for growth in capacity, in understanding, in transparency, and in the way we value the knowledge worker. All that capacity is there, untapped and unexploited. Once we let go of the limitations the old way of thinking imposed upon us, we can begin to see different ways of thinking.

This gives us the capacity to respond to the challenges the organization will face as the status quo is disrupted by the new way we engage with customers and the way customers want to interact with us. This growth is facilitated when we are able to understand that A.G.I.L.E. is a different way of thinking from the way we may have engaged very successfully in the past. The past was set up for those organizations that had very large infrastructures and a very large capacity for long-term investments. And in many organizations, those are still the parameters of success. We need the A.G.I.L.E. way of thinking when we do not know what it is the customer wants, when we must engage with knowledge workers, and when we are working in the area of high complexity and high uncertainty. We need to continue to remind ourselves that not everything we do in an enterprise requires this way of thinking; however, if we do something that fits the above description, we will find this approach beneficial in the growth we seek.

As we grow in our capacity to embrace A.G.I.L.E. thinking, we should expect some increased level of predictability as long as our approach, the way of thinking, and outputs are in alignment with the outcomes we seek. If there is no alignment or if we are only applying agile terminology or rolling out agile in a plan-driven approach, we should not expect to see the predictability of creative output that we seek.

There is no reason an A.G.I.L.E. way of thinking should be expected to bring predictability to the plan-driven approach that has been so much a part of our largest organizations since the dawn of the industrial age. The growth and sophistication of the plan-driven approach to produce deliverables is well understood; it is the inability of those deliverables to tie to the desired outcomes that has allowed A.G.I.L.E. to become popular. In a faster moving environment, we need to make the shift where necessary, in a full-throated way, to the A.G.I.L.E. way of thinking. This shift may be very uncomfortable for those leading the organizations that need it most. Unfortunately, they are also the very leaders that will need to push down control.

> The leader who has grown and is able to push control back to the people that are closest to the work and most knowledgeable about the work will need to lead the way on product development.

This does not mean that there should be less accountability; it actually means that there is an opportunity for more. Accountability is a significant opportunity for growth as we push down control to the lowest levels of the decision-making and risk-management functions within a product.

> Predictability happens with the ability to deliver output; however, the outcomes will remain dependent on the insights of those setting the strategy and product direction.

The "what" and "how" are separated, as well as the "how much", so teams can focus on the how. It stands to reason that when we have better alignment among the context of the problem, the type of workers we engage and the outcomes we seek we will have more predictability.

The results come from the alignment of the leader's ability to discern the direction of the market and to balance the expectations of predictability when embracing A.G.I.L.E. thinking. We want predictability and we don't; it is the thing we want until we have it, and then it is the thing we do not want. In other words, too much predictability, which is all we wanted in the plan-driven approach, will extinguish any hope of growth in A.G.I.L.E. thinking. It is simply too easy for people to gain predictability and lose sight of the need for product success in the marketplace.

Leaders will play a pivotal role in regard to how much growth is allowed in the A.G.I.L.E. approach by how they reward, encourage, and respond when they do not get the predictability they so desperately seek, at least at the beginning of the journey.

If leaders can begin to satisfy themselves with the idea that they are doing the next best thing for the product, that is the most they can do in a *highly complex, highly uncertain* environment. If the environment is neither of those things, there may be good reason not to embrace the A.G.I.L.E. way of thinking.

The balance will be decided as the journey unfolds; however, many will not get to this point because it is too uncomfortable for those who would rather be right than successful.

Once we have committed to the growth of A.G.I.L.E. thinking, we need to accelerate at a pace that will allow for learning through failure so that it is talked about in an open and productive way. The acceleration will allow for quicker learning cycles that will be imprinted on the people who experience the learning. Since A.G.I.L.E. thinking is empirical, people will struggle to learn it if they do not experience it. The idea of immersion is a good way for people to be exposed to A.G.I.L.E. If, however, it is in a context within their day-to-day role, they will most likely fall back quickly to the plan-driven approach and then focus more on predictability. Predictability is the club that has been used to apply immense pressure to achieve results in the plan-driven approach, but it is not what has delivered the desired outcomes.

When we do not want predictability, we seek acceleration. If we are not going faster, what is the benefit of this investment in a new way of thinking?

This does not mean we are not sustainable or predictable; it means we are growing incrementally in all of our capabilities. The acceleration efforts must be tempered by the idea that we are not trying to apply external pressure on the people doing the work; we are very good at that approach in the plan-driven model, and we see the results in how creative and productive people are when they are under stress. This plan-driven approach is useful when we have discrete tasks to accomplish; however, when we create products that need to work holistically, we will need to think in a way that allows for the sustainability of creative endeavors. This concept is new to many in the large enterprise setting since the functional, disintegration of roles is modeled after the industrial age approach to discrete work. Discrete work does not create the experience that many seek in their interaction with our enterprises today.

With A.G.I.L.E., we are growing in the way we interact with each other, with the product, and with the customer.

As we begin to understand more and more about how to think in an A.G.I.L.E. way, we develop the ability to bring together cross-functional teams and not be as discrete in our organizational approach based on skill set or function. The conversation also begins to shift and people get behind the product they are building instead of getting behind a function. This is another growth opportunity for leaders because they will be the ones that reward this new approach to work, seek out those that embrace the A.G.I.L.E. way of thinking, and allow others to see these rewards for being pioneers in the arena.

While we focus on the results that are seen in the product we produce, we must apply our growth to the capability of the team in order to keep growing. This means that leaders must either continue to develop their A.G.I.L.E. thinking or run the risk of being run over by the team or hindering the momentum that the team produces. The acceleration will come with the right people being brought together and allowing them to become a long-lived, high-performing team. Long-lived means months and years, not days and weeks. Again, the tendency of managers to manage by moving resources to the work and optimizing utilization is not how A.G.I.L.E. happens.

Although many of the constructs of the plan-driven approach become impediments to the A.G.I.L.E. way of thinking, they remain useful to the plan-driven approach for producing deliverables. They are there in support of a different way of producing outputs and may very well hinder A.G.I.L.E. thinking. Without the ability and desire to question everything, A.G.I.L.E. will likely not grow or at least not be able to grow at a rate that will ensure the support for the empirical approach.

The benefits of thinking in an A.G.I.L.E. way will be seen in individuals first and foremost. The organizational impediments will take time to identify and remove. The individuals will need the courage to embrace the shift and risk the short-term challenges that the organizational impediments put on them and their success within the organization. It is often easy to observe behaviors that are not in alignment with the A.G.I.L.E. way of thinking and expect people to shift. This is a naïve way of approaching what can be a very challenging and personal shift. It is especially challenging for those that have achieved a level of success using a different way of approaching work, namely, the plan-driven or deterministic approach. It is likely that the people who will be willing to embrace this approach will be newer to the organization, not as encumbered by status or reputation, and may be more passionate about the customer and their satisfaction. They will be more likely to question everything, and it will take commitment from the leaders that are growing in their A.G.I.L.E. thinking to help them understand which impediments may take longer than others to address. The leader will need to reflect on a regular basis to ensure that they are demonstrating the courage to address the next most important impediments and not just providing excuses for the organization to maintain the status quo.

As individuals begin to interact differently, they will be challenged by every organizational impediment.

Knowledge workers must see movement from their leaders to stay the course on the growth journey to this A.G.I.L.E. way of thinking. This is a behavioral change that requires people to show up differently than they have in the past and will create anxiety for those experimenting with this new thought process. It is easy to derail the opportunity for growth by expecting this to be easy, especially in well-established, large organizations that have had great success with the plan-driven deterministic approach.

Organizations are designed to maintain the status quo to ensure stability. However, when an organization seeks to begin thinking and working in a more A.G.I.L.E. way, it must understand that the organization is not its friend. As discussed, the impediments to thinking in a more A.G.I.L.E. way are the very things that enable the organization to be stable.

As individuals become aware of changes in themselves, they will need to monitor how these changes are received by and impact the team they are a part of. The reality is that most of what we do today cannot be done alone. We need to produce the products that drive the outcomes we seek at a complex pace and level; in order to accomplish this and deliver the outcomes we desire, we will need a team, and possibly many teams, as we move from the plan-driven approach to the empirical approach. We will need to pay attention to how people are embracing and maturing in the A.G.I.L.E. way of thinking if we are to enable growth once its begun. This is a specific role that is critical for the success we seek. The awareness of individuals of these good changes or the resistance that these changes create must be addressed, or they will become the new impediments. When open to this awareness in themselves and the observation of it in others, people are able to see the lack of that same behavior in other team members, resulting in a rich environment for experiential learning.

The growth of the customer may be the hardest growth opportunity to break through and, depending on the product being produced, it may come sooner or later compared with other areas of growth.

A.G.I.L.E. thinking shows up in results for the customer, which may take some time as we have had to produce output along the way to get to where the customer will see the benefits of this new approach. Many customers may like the plan-driven approach for the way they receive their product. It is easier for the customer to reject work when they have not been part of the development. It is also easier for them to be critical when we maintain an *us* and *them* mentality; however, this is not the approach that A.G.I.L.E. thinking supports.

How can we tell whether our customers will even value agile as we may as an organization? The customer is used to showing up in a certain respect to your product. Will they have the energy or desire to interact in a new and different way, or will they prefer to play the same role in the same way? The value we deliver through the A.G.I.L.E. way of thinking will be different; however, it may not be desired by your current customer. If the current customer is not giving you feedback that you need to change, why are you changing? The customer should be the driver for the shift, although maybe not directly; however, we should be able to justify the investment and the challenges to the organization by at least making an empirical argument as to why we are making the shift to grow in the A.G.I.L.E. way of thinking.

What is the burning platform on which such a significant change in approach is warranted?

This needs to be carefully considered, as this will be a significant investment in time, resources, and mental energy and will be a journey that will not happen quickly. We are talking years and not months for any organization at scale to make the change. The shift in thinking will be observable and valuable once embraced. The customer, whether internal or external, should be one of the first to see the value. Ultimately, the customer should see the value of this new way of thinking through the product.

**Reflection:**
1. How will rewards change in an agile environment?
2. How does acceleration help people begin to use these new approaches to work?
3. What role does self-reflection play in embracing this new way of thinking?

Adaptability
Growth
Improvement
Leadership
Experience

# Improvement

**Objectives:**
1. Understand the relationship between improvement and outcomes.
2. Determine the parameters of improvement.
3. Consider the different aspects of improvement in the nonphysical world.

There is a momentum that occurs when we begin to think in an A.G.I.L.E. way that is almost magical in its output and outcomes. However, if we do not generate that momentum and allow failure to occur without learning, we will have a hard time improving. If this happens, we are likely to fall into managing the situation, improvement will not be as rapid, and the commitment to thinking differently will be lost.

Remember that there are no best practices for creating complex products; there are only better practices.

We need to give up on predictability of outcome and focus on improving. When working in an A.G.I.L.E. way, improving is our constant companion. The question that should be continually asked is, "What are we focusing on to improve at any particular time?" The sensing and response cycle will determine what the focus is for a given time frame. We tend to either allow for improvement to take too long, seek too much improvement, or do not allow enough time for improvement to occur. Balance is needed in order to create an observable amount of improvement that will be recognized as valuable by the people paying for and using the improvement. In the digital age, we improve by getting better at giving the user or customer something they want more quickly with all of the quality parameters needed for them to be willing to use the improvement. If the improvement is not observable or discernible, the value will not register with those who have paid for it or those who must be willing to pay for it in the future.

Improvement is actually an advanced way of thinking along the journey owing to the constructs that must be present for us to realize that we can improve, must improve, and need to improve quickly. The need for improvement without delay when working in an A.G.I.L.E. way is obvious to those who are challenged to produce innovative value on a very short cadence.

A.G.I.L.E. recognizes that we do not have a model that allows for the status quo to be the rule. Bear in mind that there are environments and organizations that should be tied strongly to a deterministic and plan-driven approach for delivering value; however, there are many organizations that, if implemented, would see a significant improvement in value delivery by working in an A.G.I.L.E. way.

How do we know where to target our improvement efforts? If we are dealing with hard science and established facts, we can be fairly certain that we can use A.G.I.L.E. to innovate with that science; however, once the innovation is conceived, we will revert to a plan-driven approach to produce the product. The physical world often dictates the way we interact with it. However, A.G.I.L.E. can be leveraged for the problem-solving activities when we are not fully constrained by the physical world. The digital world is one such example; we are not constrained by physics when we are creating the digital interactions our customers are seeking and, for the most part, the digital world is seperate from the physical. The way forward in this environment is not as constrained as it would be if we were making a physical product. This reinforces the need for faster feedback loops to ensure we can pivot as quickly as our customers are sensing and responding to our products and services. If we are synchronized with our customers, we will be able to continue to deliver the value they seek and be rewarded for that value delivery.

Improvement is the goal of the empirical method and is supported by the A.G.I.L.E. way of thinking. If we fail, we learn and have the opportunity to get better. Without the real possibility of failure, there won't be a need to get better or to seriously apply the inspect-and-adapt process to do things differently.

Organizations want and often need a level of repeatability to be able to scale well-understood processes. This is appropriate with the plan-driven context; however, when we are engaged in creative endeavors, this process becomes as useless as the plan-driven approach if we are doing things for the first time or if we do not know the exact right way to get the outcomes we seek. Why would we codify an approach in a process without knowing if it will yield the outcomes we seek?

The benefit of A.G.I.L.E. is that we are constantly learning through our actions in short cycles that allow us to get better quickly.

**Reflection:**
1. How do value and improvement interact?
2. Who are the beneficiaries of improvements?
3. How do we discern what type of environment we operate within?

Adaptability
Growth
Improvement
Leadership
Experience

# Leadership

**Objectives:**
1. Understand that leadership changes in an environment that embraces A.G.I.L.E. thinking.
2. Interpret the usefulness of hierarchy in this new environment.
3. Recognize leaders will need to reinterpret what utilization looks like.

Logically, deterministic thinking is desirable if we can have defined inputs that yield predictable outcomes; however, in instances where A.G.I.L.E. thinking is needed, we are dealing with a complex creative process that does not yield easily to the force of will, which we see often in the plan-driven approach to efforts. Leadership will need to move in a new direction if organizations are to get different results, better results, and different outcomes. The idea that it is some externally driven change we are seeking is again an old way of looking at the organization. The vast majority of agile efforts are seeking very similar outcomes that others have already achieved. In some instances, there may be some innovation at play, but creation is not taking place. Once again, it comes back to the need for a new leadership approach that allows for autonomy and agency. Without the chemistry changing, how can we see a marked difference in the output?

When we think about leading in an A.G.I.L.E. way, it is, first and foremost, a realization that hierarchy has to be put on the shelf for everything except pure coordination of activity and when there is chaos and anarchy. At the end of the day, there will need to be someone whom everyone will listen to in these extreme circumstances; however, these circumstances are a lot rarer than we think. The difference in our understanding of what these circumstances appear to be is that we have become hypersensitive based on our plan-driven mindset and allow only for that mindset to be present. If we are to lead differently to get different outcomes, we need to let go of the ingrained notion of leadership that has permeated the industrial age.

That previously ingrained mindset tells us that as we move up the hierarchy, we know more than everyone below us in the hierarchy and that we are a source of answers to solve their problem or the problems of the organization. Leadership is really about scaling; we need to scale to solve really large problems, which cannot be solved in a plan-driven deterministic manner when we do not know what the answer could or should be. We need an empirical approach to move us in the direction of the answer through experimentation. In corporate settings, experimenting is such a foreign concept, and we use inspection and adaption often to express the approach. It becomes especially difficult when we realize that when we are experimenting, we will find things that do not work or move us toward our desired outcomes. Some will see that as failure, but others will see it as learning. It is the ones that see it as learning and not just give lip service to the concept that have a real chance to lead in an A.G.I.L.E. way.

**Reflection:**
1. How critical is leadership in this journey? Why?
2. What ideas do you have that will allow an A.G.I.L.E. way of thinking to take hold without full management support?
3. What psychological barriers are there to this shift in leaders?

Adaptability
Growth
Improvement
Leadership

Experience

# Experience

**Objectives:**
1. Understand where experience lies in an organization.
2. Determine the importance of the team in collecting experience.
3. Realize that deterministic analysis cannot demonstrate the value of A.G.I.L.E. thinking.

Not all experience is created equal, and certain experiences tend to hinder our ways of thinking. We can address behavior by gaining new and different experiences within an A.G.I.L.E. way of thinking. However, it is something that needs to be embraced and not feared, and that will take the support and encouragement of the organization. Leaders will need to go first and show vulnerability. Again, this will be a huge challenge for well-established organizations that may not really embrace the need for thinking in an A.G.I.L.E. way.

Individuals are where the experience resides, and by investing in their experience, the benefits of A.G.I.L.E. thinking will be expanded. While experience is not necessary at the beginning of the journey, and at times can be undesirable, A.G.I.L.E. helps us grow in experience. We encourage continued growth by thinking in a particular way…. an A.G.I.L.E. way.

While individual experience is valuable, thinking A.G.I.L.E. as a team is where the force multiplier occurs. Without the commitment to respect the experience of high-performing teams and value that as an asset, the benefits of A.G.I.L.E. thinking will be unpredictable and short-lived. Every time the composition of a team changes, we begin again to gain a common experience on which we leverage our ability to improve as a team. The goals of resource optimization must be eliminated from the corporate lexicon if we are to capitalize on the potential of high-performing teams. The experience of the team must become its DNA in order to allow it to grow at a rapid pace through common inspection and adaption. Without the common experience, there is no foundation for trust.

The idea that A.G.I.L.E. thinking is easy or that it is undisciplined or obvious is supported only by people who have not experienced it. When stakeholders become aware of the value of A.G.I.L.E. and as it shows benefits in their area of responsibility, they are much more willing to embrace and support it. However, it is only through experience that this realization happens. Every time a team gets new stakeholders, A.G.I.L.E. thinking takes a step back, and new stakeholders must be brought along on the journey. This is why many organizations make a mistake when trying to move to an A.G.I.L.E. way of thinking when they roll it out from a top-down approach. The stakeholders have as much work to do with A.G.I.L.E. as the teams. Without this work, there is no alignment by all parties. There are mechanics of agile that can be taught and should be taught; however, A.G.I.L.E. is experienced, and the more the cohort of learners are kept intact, the more likely and quickly they will absorb this new way of thinking.

It is much easier to think about working on a product that is being created than one that has had a long history. The challenge with the A.G.I.L.E. way of thinking regarding products goes back to the challenge of experienced teams. The more we allow teams to work with a product, the more agile they become as long as A.G.I.L.E. thinking is being practiced in all its other forms, as described in the previous chapters.

**Reflection:**
1. How do we decide where best to experiment with A.G.I.L.E.?
2. What barriers will need to be overcome to allow for experience to be gained?
3. Who will be the recipient of the experience, and what will they do with it?

# PART 2

# Building on the Foundation

| A | G | I |
|---|---|---|
| Accountability | Goal | Intention |
| Alignment | | Invitation |
| Application | | Innovation |
| Attitude | | Ideas |
| Attention | | Increment |
| Action | | Information |
| Absorb | | Impact |
| Agency | | **E** |
| **L** | | Everything |
| Learning | | Experiment |
| Linking | | Empiricism |

## Accountability

**Objectives:**

1. Understand what is meant by accountability in an A.G.I.L.E. environment.
2. Describe where accountability shifts from and to in an A.G.I.L.E. environment.

Working in an A.G.I.L.E. way often changes how accountability works and how we understand what it is. Accountability has been used in many different ways to try and make sure people do what they are supposed to do and is often seen as something that happens to someone (i.e., *someone needs to be held accountable*). This type of approach is a symptom of something that happens when well-intentioned people are overwhelmed with the sheer volume of activity required. Thinking in an A.G.I.L.E. way begins to unwind the conflicts of everyday work by helping people focus and makes them more willing to be held accountable.

One of the best ways to introduce accountability is at the team level. This will begin to shift the conversation from *I* to *we the team*. In this accountability model, we invite the team to make commitments that are for a short period of time, such as 1 to 4 weeks, and the commitment is for the entire team to achieve the desired or planned outcome. In this model, we begin to break the idea that a person can be successful apart from the team. This drives the team to collaborate more and to focus their energies during these short iterations on the outcome being sought.

Working in an A.G.I.L.E. way helps drive different behavior by allowing the team to commit to a particular output over a specific period.

> While this output may or may not be of long-term value, we have the benefit of creating a focused, problem-solving team.

The *commit-focus-output* model allows for the team to embrace accountability because they understand what outputs the team will be accountable for delivering. Unfortunately, there is not a linear connection between outputs and outcomes. Outcomes come in response to the outputs of the team and require that we use feedback to make course corrections along the way to hone in on what our customers see as valuable.

> Accountability can happen only when there is:
>
> Focus
> Commitment
> Short time horizons

This model is sometimes done with the quarter over quarter of corporate earnings. While those are outcomes that do drive focus, the challenge with the corporate earning model is that it is not a shared commitment of the team, and the people that have the accountability do not always have the ability to impact the outcome in a meaningful way in such a short period. As we begin to break down the outcomes to something so small that a team can understand, commit to, and focus on, we are much more likely to be able to invite accountability by the team. In order to do this, we need to separate the *what* from the *how* of the work. However, it is very difficult for leaders who are tasked with looking outside the organization to continually look at the details of the *how* and direct each team's work. Separating the what and how allows leaders to focus on the outside environment to clearly articulate the what of the work. Once the *what* is understood, the team can focus on *how* to get the outputs. Outputs allow for feedback to come from the market. The command and control model of the industrial age has been very successful in the past when we did not have the current level of disruption in the marketplace; therefore, organizations could use the plan-driven approach and go at the pace of the leader's ability to manage the *what* and the *how*. By enabling individuals to align to teams and stay within their areas of focus, accountability is much easier to achieve, and conversations begin to take place when everyone is committed to the same outcomes.

**Reflection:**
1. How does the language change in the new accountability model?
2. What challenges do you see with people who want to be the hero that "saves the day"?

| A | G | I |
|---|---|---|
| Accountability | Goal | Intention |
| Alignment | | Invitation |
| Application | | Innovation |
| Attitude | | Ideas |
| Attention | | Increment |
| Action | | Information |
| Absorb | | Impact |
| Agency | | **E** |
| **L** | | Everything |
| Learning | | Experiment |
| Linking | | Empiricism |

## Alignment

**Objectives:**

1. Realize that alignment to an entirely new set of guiding ideas will be needed.
2. Understand that a conscious awareness will be needed to make such a shift.
3. Embrace the uncertainty that comes with an empirical approach.

Different approaches need to be aligned in order to begin thinking in an A.G.I.L.E. way. The alignment is a shift from what has worked well in the past within the plan-driven, deterministic approaches to concepts and approaches that support agile.

- Movement from the individual to the team is a significant shift for many people. Managers, as the smallest unit in people management, are often thought to be a percentage of a person, such as when we allocate 10 percent, 25 percent, or 50 percent of a person to an effort. The idea that we can allocate partial people to work is a key concept of the plan-driven approach.

This is based on the premise that we move the people to the work instead of moving the work to the people.

- Agile will shift from the project-based approach that produces deliverables to looking at products that exist for as long as people are using them. This has been driven by the digital engagement of users and the need to have platforms for ongoing and evolving engagement. Products are the output of the project; they are the end of the work.

We can no longer console ourselves with the idea that deliverables are the measure of a successful project. We must get feedback from our customers on an ongoing basis.

- Deliverables as the measure of success will be moved to the outcomes we seek as a result of the work. This is one of the biggest challenges from a human perspective. We are not sure how to get the outcomes we seek, which is why we are using agile. However, it is hard to feel good about outcomes in the moment because they are not obvious.
- We move from deterministic (plan-driven) to empirical because we need to have an experiment-based approach to achieving the outcomes we seek. This goes hand in hand with the realization that we do not know how to achieve the outcomes we seek, so an empirical approach is needed.
- We move from a perception of certainty, however false it may be, to the reality of the uncertainty of not being in control of the market, customer, or, in many cases, the perceived experience of the customer. This will continue to create uncertainty, producing a need to be empirical in our approach, where we are continuously inspecting and adapting.
- We move from thinking that creative work is simple or complicated and begin to understand the complexity of the creative process so that we can embrace the appropriate problem-solving models, as described earlier.

The intention around alignment will come up over and over again in this book. These are well-worn patterns in our minds and will take deliberate and purposeful thought to begin to shift toward A.G.I.L.E. thinking.

**Reflection:**

1. What ideas do you have that will help us make the needed shifts toward an A.G.I.L.E. way of thinking?
2. How important will these shifts be in seeing the outcomes we seek to become more A.G.I.L.E.?
3. What might be some of the first behaviors that we see return when we do not see the outcomes we seek?

| **A** | **G** | **I** |
|---|---|---|
| Accountability | Goal | Intention |
| Alignment | | Invitation |
| Application | | Innovation |
| Attitude | | Ideas |
| Attention | | Increment |
| Action | | Information |
| Absorb | | Impact |
| Agency | | **E** |
| **L** | | Everything |
| Learning | | Experiment |
| Linking | | Empiricism |

## Application

**Objectives:**
1. Determine the best experiments for an A.G.I.L.E. way of thinking.
2. Ensure they are well suited to this approach and not set up for failure.
3. Realize not all environments are suited to this approach.

The proper application of this new way of thinking will take some analysis and understanding of the problem domain under consideration. If we try applying this new way of thinking to every problem set, we will frustrate the process we endeavor to use and the outcomes we seek. This is not a silver bullet to be applied in every circumstance. It will yield the desired improvements only when it cannot be determined with certainty what will satisfy the customer or how to yield the outcomes needed. This is much more than an organizational alignment. It is not unusual that organizations approach it as such since that is how change has been inflicted on organizations for at least the last 50 years. This was appropriate because the way work was done did not change. Since our interest is no longer in controlling the work, we need to fundamentally change the way the work flows and who determines how the work is performed. This can only be effective if we have the alignment spoken about in other parts of this book.

We will need to experiment with which circumstances will benefit from the application of the A.G.I.L.E. way of thinking. There are well-known sweet spots that we should start with when exploring A.G.I.L.E. thinking inside of an organization; however, we should also be open to novel ideas in areas that have not yielded to the more plan-driven approach to work in the past.

Application is the taking of action in a certain direction and is the basis for the experimentation needed. Be careful with the application space and how well the empirical approach is applied, which is the foundation of A.G.I.L.E thinking. The more we allow the plan-driven deterministic approach to remain in force, the less we can evaluate the merits of our efforts.

Application will not be demonstrated with a shift in terminology the way many change initiatives are deemed a success or failure, nor will training yield the result that the proper application through experimentation would. Training can only serve as an introduction to the A.G.I.L.E. ways of working. The real introduction is its use, in context, with a team using the empirical approach to problem-solving.

**Reflections:**
1. Consider what might make a good use case for experimentation.
2. Consider what might not make a good use case for the A.G.I.L.E. way of thinking.
3. Consider at least one novel use case for an experiment.

| **A** | **G** | **I** |
|---|---|---|
| Accountability | Goal | Intention |
| Alignment | | Invitation |
| Application | | Innovation |
| Attitude | | Ideas |
| Attention | | Increment |
| Action | | Information |
| Absorb | | Impact |
| Agency | | **E** |
| **L** | | Everything |
| Learning | | Experiment |
| Linking | | Empiricism |

## Attitude

**Objectives:**

1. Understand that an attitude founded in growth and experimentations is needed.
2. Realize we will need to seek new information to navigate in this new way.
3. Determine to challenge the well-worn behavior patterns of the plan-driven approach.

Thinking in an A.G.I.L.E. way requires a shift in attitude so that we look at things with a fresh set of eyes and without all the plan-driven deterministic models that have served us so well. Without this awareness, people will believe that all of the tools and techniques, even the terminology of a plan-driven approach, is readily transferable to agile. Fortunately, many of the facilitation and collaboration techniques that have been taught, and sometimes rarely used, are highly transferable. An attitude grounded in growth and experimentation is the foundation needed.

The attitude that we know, and have used successfully, must be suspended in order to inspect and adapt our way to success in this new model. If we lack the awareness that a new attitude needs to be present, we will miss the opportunities that A.G.I.L.E. presents. When we arrive in a new city, we notice more and have an increased awareness of our surroundings. This is because we are not sure what we need to give attention to, so our curiosity is higher, as well as our anxiety at times. If we treat the agile journey as a trip to a new city, we will be better prepared to observe and report along the way what we are seeing, hearing, feeling, doing, and thinking. With this information coming back into our feedback cycle, we will be better prepared to know what to do next.

The lack of this fundamental shift in attitude will pose the greatest risks to the potential benefits to be realized by working in an A.G.I.L.E. way. There is evidence that we have already begun to lose the benefit proposition because we have not sufficiently changed the status quo in our own attitudes, let alone in our organizations. This is likely because well-respected and well-compensated consultants who do not understand the attitude but can replicate the mechanics are telling leaders this is how it is done. That is not how we shift attitudes, and therefore we become more likely to spend enormous sums, while creating a lot of organizational churn without the attitude shift needed.

Without the new attitude, we are likely to continue to request the same information, interpret it the same way, and make use of the same decision patterns that have been so well established by working in a deterministic plan-driven world. These are well-worn behavior patterns that must be consciously and continually challenged if we are to reap the benefits of A.G.I.L.E.

**Reflection:**

1. In what ways can we continue to challenge the status quo once the shift begins?
2. How can we effectively counsel the need to go slow at first to allow the attitude shift to begin?
3. What characteristics best indicate where there may be fertile ground for an experiment to be run?

| **A** | **G** | **I** |
|---|---|---|
| Accountability | Goal | Intention |
| Alignment | | Invitation |
| Application | | Innovation |
| Attitude | | Ideas |
| Attention | | Increment |
| Action | | Information |
| Absorb | | Impact |
| Agency | | **E** |
| **L** | | Everything |
| Learning | | Experiment |
| Linking | | Empiricism |

## Attention

**Objectives:**
1. Determine what model works for which situation.
2. Understand the role of the team and the role of the individual.
3. Gain insight into how to continue to develop a higher performing team.

With a new attitude, we will be able to give attention to different things that may have been present in the past but may not have been useful in a plan-driven environment. The reality of moving people to the work in a plan-driven approach makes sense if resource utilization was what we were after. This was the old model of the industrial age, when we needed to reduce and specialize each worker's tasks so the outcomes could become more and more predictable. This was the only way we could evaluate the worker and determine who was doing well and who was not. Working in an A.G.I.L.E. way will have us pay more attention to the team level of engagement and refrain from looking at the individual as a unit of production. This is a difficult shift and will require leaders to pay attention to what they focus on, as we have always focused on getting the most out of individuals and evaluating people as the unit of production. A.G.I.L.E. is a way to get knowledge workers functioning as a high-performing team, which will need to work toward bettering their overall output over time.

The role of the leader becomes critical in the selection process of talent for the team and will need to be strongly focused on each individual's teaming skills if we are to progress quickly toward becoming a high-performing team. While we will need specialists, this is another potential pitfall in how we roll out A.G.I.L.E.; as we have mentioned, there is no such thing as "one size fits all", and there may need to be individual contributors who have deep expertise that many teams use. This means we need to allow that team member to be an individual and flow the work to her. This should be the exception more than the rule as we begin to return to the craftsman model as it applies to teams. Production line specialization works when we know exactly what we are building and how we will build it. Absent that certainty, we need to use collaboration of people to solve the numerous problems that present themselves when we are doing things for the first time.

This shift in attention will create a delicate inflection point as organizations begin this journey since people were not hired for this type of environment. This means that everyone will be changing how, how much, and with whom they interact. There are many tools to help guide the leader in this environment, and they become more and more mature as automation takes over more of the repetitive tasks, freeing us to create and innovate in an A.G.I.L.E. way. This is where the ability to use emotional intelligence (EI) assessments will be of great benefit to the leader. These, as well as skill-based or personality tools, can be combined in a tool like cloverleaf.me to give leaders insight into how to build teams beyond the narrow hard skills approach. The personality-based evaluations become critical in the A.G.I.L.E. world as we are asking teams to work and deliver what individuals cannot. Leaders will struggle to shift away from resource and task management to paying attention to the composition of the team and away from placing the work in the hands of the most qualified person to do the work. Again, resource optimization is not the role of the leader in this new way of working. The leader now needs to look for impediments that are hindering the entire team from being more productive. It is not even the leader's role to determine what will be the output; it is the leader's role to clearly define the outcomes the teams are going after. Paying attention to whom we invite to the team will go a long way in ensuring that we are paying attention to the right things when using the A.G.I.L.E. approach. The building of the high-performing team will still take a significant amount of time; however, by focusing more at the beginning, we are stacking the deck in our favor.

This approach drives the reevaluation of some of the cost optimization approaches we have taken over the last decade when developing products. Some of the more troublesome approaches to an A.G.I.L.E. way of thinking are as follows:

- Short-term workers
- Moving people on and off teams
- Funding projects, instead of teams
- Differentiating teams by design, development, or test, regardless of the product type
- Not investing in developing cross-skilled individuals
- The idea that the exact right person must do the work

While all of these approaches have been used and are used to manage operations effectively, they do not support the ongoing creation of business value as they are designed to optimize for cost and utilization.

**Reflections:**
1. How do we persuade leaders that innovation comes from different approaches?
2. How will we demonstrate compelling evidence that empiricism works for the use case under evaluation?
3. How can someone without experience in A.G.I.L.E. thinking convince others of its viability?

| **A** | **G** | **I** |
|---|---|---|
| Accountability | Goal | Intention |
| Alignment | | Invitation |
| Application | | Innovation |
| Attitude | | Ideas |
| Attention | | Increment |
| Action | | Information |
| Absorb | | Impact |
| Agency | | **E** |
| **L** | | Everything |
| Learning | | Experiment |
| Linking | | Empiricism |

## Action

**Objectives:**
1. Determine how to take smaller actions with less uncertainty.
2. Let go of the idea of resource utilization.
3. Let go of the stress of determining a plan when we know the least.

Working in an A.G.I.L.E. way requires us to rethink the actions we take and the pace at which we take them. This does not mean we will be pushing people to *do more with less;* we have already seen that play itself out in the corporate vernacular. We are saying that we *will be doing less so we can do more* and deliver more value.

The idea of doing less will make many uncomfortable and will require us to risk being wrong—not wrong in a final, no chance of recovering type of way of being wrong, but in a way that we learn and adapt to the feedback. In a plan-driven approach, we were driven to make sure we stayed on plan regardless of the plan being appropriate for the information we currently had at hand. This has conditioned many to avoid even the possibility of being wrong, of failing at an objective, or making a mistake. This is especially difficult if you have risen within an organization by not failing, or at least being perceived as not having failed. In the past, this behavior may have protected managers from unforced errors in operation, risk, or exploration; however, with the current pace of innovation and the disruption that markets are experiencing, many organizations cannot allow themselves to operate in a protective posture. The barriers to entry are not of the bygone era when massive amounts of capital were needed to challenge a competitor. And often we can prove out an idea before we need to scale, especially if it is of a digital nature.

The barriers to entry are becoming lower and lower for organizations that focus on becoming the best within a very narrow niche. They have the access to customers at an unprecedented rate, and the barriers to entry are lower for initial contact with new customers.

The action we take today will have an impact faster than ever before, and we will need to *pivot without mercy* to respond to the feedback we are experiencing. If managers begin to act when they should, before the *last responsible moment* and not the *last possible moment*, the feedback will come, and the approach will become clearer. It is not that we need to know what the customer wants and what they will be willing to pay for. We will be able to get the feedback as we operate with A.G.I.L.E. to ensure we are having many small learning cycles, and we will continue to appeal to the customer's changing preferences. This approach does not change if we seek to satisfy internal or external customers; we still need to have the same short cycles of action and feedback to ensure we are not getting outside the cone of value, as perceived by the person paying for our product or service. This will work only if we have a good relationship with getting things wrong and staying focused on the outcomes. The corporate psyche is not yet comfortable with this approach, and that is why small experiments are better than large-scale change initiatives. Many organizations have time, and they do not need to change quickly; however, they do need to change effectively because at some point they may run out of time to innovate.

By producing smaller actions more often, we can experiment and get feedback quickly to inform the next action. This is not a new concept, nor does it require a specific skill. It does, however, require a bias toward action. This bias can be cultivated and will need to be developed over time. Thinking in an A.G.I.L.E. way allows for this to take place by beginning to shorten the horizon for action, which, by definition, will cause us to do less in a particular period of time. This also has the benefit of creating a sense of urgency, which is the foundation for any change. Once the urgency is present, this will allow for the focus to meet objectives in shorter cycles of effort.

By focusing, we can achieve more than by attempting to *multitask*. This is particularly true when we are working on highly complex and highly uncertain endeavors. This is even more critical when we are working with a group of people. The propensity to get distracted is higher when we have not done something before, and it is higher if we are not constantly being active. This may be counterintuitive, given that we are speaking about action; however, what we need is action toward the goal we have committed to as a team instead of activity that allows us, as individuals, to appear productive when we are not being productive toward the goal.

The A.G.I.L.E. way of thinking does not optimize the utilization of people, referred to generically in the plan-driven approach as resources. The value delivered with A.G.I.L.E. is easier to evaluate. If an organization aspires to ensure maximum utilization at the individual level, it will be disappointed with an agile approach. The A.G.I.L.E. way of thinking does enable a more likely output at the end of a short cycle by ensuring everyone is focused on the commitment made at the beginning of the cycle. This will sometimes mean that some people on the team are doing less from time to time. As the team becomes better at planning for small cycles of work and as they start to understand how each of the team members can contribute as cross-skilled individuals to the goal, the idle time of a particular team member will be reduced.

The A.G.I.L.E. way of working requires that we leave behind the idea that we move the work to the person who can do it best or most efficiently.

It may seem like waste if we do change the way we flow work and seek the effective creation of a solution; however, the efficiency of resources is what the traditional plan-driven approach is focused on. This is often very valuable for work that is either simple or complicated; however, this approach falls down when we get into the realm of complexity. It is for this reason that A.G.I.L.E thinking is becoming more popular. Be aware, though, that just because it has become popular does not mean it is easy to understand or to practice.

By doing less, we will be able to be more committed and better able to focus on what is perceived as the most valuable thing.

When we begin thinking in an A.G.I.L.E. way, we allow for the highly complex and uncertain endeavor to reveal itself over time and free ourselves from needing to make decisions with insufficient information. The traditional demand to make decisions prematurely exerts stress on the individual, team, and organization as a whole, without delivering outcomes. How could it not when we are making these bets when uncertainty is the highest? If we begin to focus on fewer outcomes over a shorter period, we free the system up to produce an outcome that can be evaluated and for feedback to be received. The need for short feedback loops, focus, and commitments that are understood are all able to be leveraged into specific actions that can be evaluated quickly. This is truly the value of working with agile that cannot be realized any other way.

Action has different phases, and initial action is the hardest to occur. It has to overcome inertia and the natural concern of taking the wrong action. Often, we are forced to take initial action over and over, and there may be no flow to the action. When we begin working in a more A.G.I.L.E. way, we take continued action in the direction of the desired outcomes. This action begins to flow from one experiment to another with the feedback loops being the lubricant of the continuing action. There is no need to stop and think for long periods of time, as we do with initial action. We are in action, which allows us to pivot when necessary or to confirm and continue on very short intervals. Without movement we cannot pivot.

The intervals need to be long enough to enable you to produce something that can be evaluated without allowing too much time to go by in case the direction of the outcome needs to be adjusted.

There is no single right answer, and the interval is easily determined as the conversation is observed. If the interval is too short, the feedback will be unengaged. If the interval is too long, it will result in too much waste because the direction was skewed. But if it is just right, there will be acknowledgment of the results with enough feedback to allow for the next most valuable thing to be produced.

**Reflection:**
1. How can we determine the right feedback cycle time?
2. When should decisions be made when using A.G.I.L.E. thinking?
3. What are some of the inherent challenges with taking action?

| A | G | I |
|---|---|---|
| Accountability | Goal | Intention |
| Alignment | | Invitation |
| Application | | Innovation |
| Attitude | | Ideas |
| Attention | | Increment |
| Action | | Information |
| Absorb | | Impact |
| Agency | | **E** |
| **L** | | Everything |
| Learning | | Experiment |
| Linking | | Empiricism |

## Absorb

**Objectives:**

1. Notice that it takes time for people to absorb their newfound autonomy.
2. Realize that autonomy is not the only ingredient to the A.G.I.L.E. way of thinking at the individual level.
3. Understand that the organizational pull to revert to old behaviors will be strong for many years.

The absorption rate of incorporating A.G.I.L.E. into an organization will depend on how much capacity there is within the system to allow for the new way of thinking. If there are already too many things that are in play for the existing system to absorb, this new way of thinking will be just another one of those things that get little attention. It will most likely get even less attention because it will take significant mental energy for each person. This is contrary to most initiatives within the enterprise, as they are well digested by the organization before it is introduced to the individual.

Unfortunately, A.G.I.L.E. thinking can only be supported by the organization; that is, organizations do not become agile but support the individuals making the shift to thinking in an A.G.I.L.E. way.

It is then the synergistic effects that are provided by the change in people that lead to the outcomes sought by organizations.

This absorption happens at the individual level and determines whether someone will or will not allow themselves to experiment with this new approach. If the individual has a well-defined deterministic mindset, they will struggle to gain awareness that the organization is serious about the change, if indeed the organization is serious. They are more likely to only absorb what is needed to support the organizational level of change and shield themselves from absorbing the change and internalizing it.

The absorption challenge explains why we can see the obvious benefits of A.G.I.L.E. being exhibited within organizations that have grown up with this thinking; conversely, we see many very well-established organizations that have operated in the plan-driven approach for decades and even centuries struggling to see the absorption of A.G.I.L.E. thinking.

The need for a strong pull is the key for many organizations to make the shift in the appropriate areas to the A.G.I.L.E. way of thinking. The pull will need to sustain and outlast the resistance of the organization and the individuals in order to make the shift.

This shift can be enhanced by working as a group in an A.G.I.L.E. way. This is where all the really powerful and creative events happen. When we are sensing and responding to feedback from experimentation, we need to have a sense of autonomy and the ability to act within our sphere to ensure we are not hindered in our ability to pivot in the direction of the input we are receiving. So often when we are not thinking in an A.G.I.L.E. way or when we are not even allowed to do so, we do not have autonomy and are leaving the greatest ideas out of the conversation. Without the awareness of autonomy, the next step in the process of creating based on an empirical approach cannot be taken. This step occurs once we have all parties convinced that they do have autonomy. Autonomy is a necessary, though insufficient, state for the A.G.I.L.E. way of thinking to be embraced; it is agency that will enable A.G.I.L.E. thinking to take off. Agency is an individual deciding to take action as part of the team in the direction of the outcomes we seek.

**Reflection:**

1. How do we overcome the organizational pull of well-established organizations?
2. What types of organizations might have an easier time resisting the organizational pull?
3. How might people from outside the organization lend support to the desired shift?

| A | G | I |
|---|---|---|
| Accountability | Goal | Intention |
| Alignment | | Invitation |
| Application | | Innovation |
| Attitude | | Ideas |
| Attention | | Increment |
| Action | | Information |
| Absorb | | Impact |
| Agency | | **E** |
| **L** | | Everything |
| Learning | | Experiment |
| Linking | | Empiricism |

## Agency

**Objectives:**

1. Understand that agency is difficult in well-established organizations.
2. Realize that small teams are the best place to develop agency.
3. Decide what is the proper role of traditional change management approaches on the A.G.I.L.E. journey.

Agency is even more important than autonomy and critical to the journey to A.G.I.L.E. Oftentimes, there has been a realization within the environment that A.G.I.L.E. thinking is needed and is being pursued in an authentic way, but the people who do have autonomy within the structure are still operating as if they do not. The ability to embrace agency, defined as the willingness to act on autonomy, is the next awareness that needs to be brought forward and supported. In organizations that have long-standing patterns of behavior that were not in keeping with A.G.I.L.E. thinking, people will struggle with this shift because of the behaviors they have picked up through the predominant culture. It is learned helplessness at an organizational level that must be faced and is something that must be explored first at the local level within small teams. A high level of trust must be built within the team for individuals to experiment with new ways of working and thinking.

We cannot force agency at any level, so we must invite it and provide an environment for people to begin to experiment with it. There is often a sense that this approach takes too long and that there must be a plan-driven approach to make this happen on a schedule.

What if we incentivize people?
What can we measure?
Should we bring in a big consulting firm?

Surely, all of these approaches have been tried, and we are hopeful that when everything else has been tried, we will allow autonomy and agency to grow out of small, self-organizing teams to lead us to the A.G.I.L.E. way of thinking.

If we see otherwise bright, dedicated individuals reluctant to act, we are most likely going to struggle to convince them that they do have autonomy and the support of the culture to act on that autonomy through agency to experiment, get feedback, pivot, sense, and respond. This cycle shouldn't end as long as business value is being delivered within the product or capability. The outcomes and the way of achieving them are uncertain, so we will need to get comfortable with the sense and respond cycle in order to make the changes that other organizations will be making to achieve success.

If we begin to see the seeds of autonomy and agency emerging, we will need to be very careful to nurture them. The first response to failure will determine whether there is any indication that the organization is willing to support the true change that is required to support A.G.I.L.E. The A.G.I.L.E. way of thinking is certainly a challenge for individuals; however, for large, well-established organizations, there will be a significant need for shifts in the actions, behaviors, and consequences through the journey.

Our plan-driven mindset has conditioned us to use people to get things done, instead of supporting people to do what needs to be done.

The idea of using people is so prevalent in the plan-driven terminology because we see everything as a resource and must realize that just because we stop calling people *resources,* we have not shifted to thinking in an A.G.I.L.E. way.

The idea that we can replicate what is being done in very nimble and new organizations in large established organizations is not likely to result in people working in a more A.G.I.L.E. way. On the other hand, thinking that we can implement A.G.I.L.E. thinking the same way that we implement other change initiatives is just as naive. There is a need for someone who has gone on the journey to be a guide to others. A common approach is to hire or engage people who have been part of an *agile transformation* to do it for another organization from a very senior level, but this approach is often not useful. People from the outside will struggle with context and not be close enough to the inherent impediments to change what exists organically within the organization. One approach that holds promise is to engage experienced A.G.I.L.E. thinkers and partner them with people who want to experience the journey. This is much more intense than the classic executive leadership coaching model, but similar in other regards.

Unfortunately, organizations approach this type of change like all other types of change and often see few benefits and little, if any, shift in thinking. Many of the advocates of this new way of thinking and interacting do not have the ability to contrast what needs to be different at scale because they have not been a part of or led other types of organizational change, specifically a shift from the plan-driven model to the empirical model. While moving to an A.G.I.L.E. way of thinking is different than other changes, there is an ability to compare a need for a different approach to how we engage with this type of initiative.

Inviting a new way of thinking is very different than other change initiatives that have often taken place within these well-established organizations that have not grown up digital. The other changes have been about process or tool changes. There have been many organizations that have used traditional approaches to change or that implement new computer systems like SAP. Having personally been a part of many of these changes, they are simple compared with what is being attempted by inviting people, teams, and entire organizations to think in an A.G.I.L.E. way.

Think of the wagon trainmaster that would guide wagon trains for months to the West Coast across the vast western part of the United States. Not everyone had a wagon trainmaster, not everyone took a wagon train, and even those that took one did not always make it to the west. However, riding on the wagon train was the most likely way to have success. Similarly, if you are thinking that this will be a mechanical exercise, you will be disappointed with your results. The mechanics can help model the behaviors and interactions that A.G.I.L.E. thinking brings about, but unless you are embracing the thinking constructs of A.G.I.L.E., the mechanics will most likely have a negative impact on the outcomes for which you are embarking on this journey.

There have been well-defined roles that have allowed us to facilitate change in organizations; however, those roles have been skill based in nature. With A.G.I.L.E., we fundamentally shift the way we think, which has been uncharacteristic of large organizations emerging out of the industrial age. This is primarily because it was not needed, and the more plan-driven deterministic models continue to be successful mostly in cases when we are not seeking to change the very way people think.

**Reflection:**
1. How best do we support the shift needed in the way people think?
2. What can individuals do to embrace this journey of change?
3. What role do traditional change models have in the shift to the A.G.I.L.E. way of thinking?

| A | G | I |
|---|---|---|
| Accountability | Goal | Intention |
| Alignment | | Invitation |
| Application | | Innovation |
| Attitude | | Ideas |
| Attention | | Increment |
| Action | | Information |
| Absorb | | Impact |
| Agency | | **E** |
| **L** | | Everything |
| Learning | | Experiment |
| Linking | | Empiricism |

## Goal

**Objectives:**
1. Understand the role of common goals for bringing people together.
2. Realize who is responsible for determining the difficulty of the goal.
3. Harmonize goals and outcome-based focus.

Goals need to exist for the organization, team, and product. We need to embrace empirical goals that allow for failure. Without the very real possibility of failure, we will not be able to grow and absorb more of the empirical learning we seek by embracing A.G.I.L.E. thinking. The possibility of failure must exist for people to come together and seek common understanding and collaboration. Goals have been used to judge performance in the past so people in the plan-driven approach have figured out how to ensure they can reach their goals. We are shifting the very definition of goals to be more of a statement of what we seek as a group. We commit everyone in the group to pursue that goal for the period we are in. The goal gets to be reevaluated at regular intervals, and the inspection will allow us to adapt our approach.

The arbitrary evaluation of the goal as easy or hard will not have the desired outcome, as this is the construct of the plan-driven approach. The goal and its potential for failure is the evaluation of those committing to its pursuit. Once committed to the goal, it becomes the beacon to focus on and rally around. The goal now has the power to begin to shift people away from a functional expertise or department and toward the common goal of the team. Action is now directed toward the goal that has been committed to by the group.

Focusing on the intent of the goal will help us see them as outcomes we seek over time through empiricism. Working in a more A.G.I.L.E. way will require an increased focus on intent since we no longer live and die by a plan; we must have a direction we are heading in at any point in time, no matter how short lived. If we need a goal for a very short interaction, we need to align to our heading so we can tell if we are off course. If we have lost sight of the goal, we can hold each other accountable to get us back on course. When we lived in a plan-driven world, we had the opportunity to be on auto pilot and not focus on intent as much. We deluded ourselves into thinking that we could, if we wanted to, hold every variable constant while we focused exclusively on the results of the plan. This has become less and less likely, especially in complex and uncertain endeavors. The map is not the terrain, and that is what the plan-driven approach allowed us to misunderstand. The empirical approach and the A.G.I.L.E. way of thinking keep us grounded and do not allow us, for long at least, to make the mistakes that the plan-driven approach made by allowing us to just look at the plan.

With an increased focus on intent, we will have the opportunity to pivot quickly and take the appropriate action without the constraint of a published, long-lived plan, where any change to it will need to be communicated to all stakeholders. The communication cycles in A.G.I.L.E. are like all other feedback loops in agile and happen on cadence and in short order to ensure we are sensing our environment and responding so that our efforts are instrumental in delivering the desired outcomes.

This is contrary to how we tend to perform within a plan-driven environment. We want to be controlled by the plan because most of our experiences indicate we do not need to iterate or pivot during its execution. This allows for optimization of execution and allows the outputs to be delivered in a more systematic and predictable manner. It does not, however, ensure that the value will be delivered. In reality, we will not know if value is delivered because we are unable to get feedback from the customer until the plan is fully executed.

**Reflection:**
1. How can we reintroduce people to the idea of goals?
2. Who gives the goal, and who needs to understand the intent behind the goal?
3. How do goals, intent, and outcomes play together?

| A | G | I |
|---|---|---|
| Accountability | Goal | Intention |
| Alignment | | Invitation |
| Application | | Innovation |
| Attitude | | Ideas |
| Attention | | Increment |
| Action | | Information |
| Absorb | | Impact |
| Agency | | **E** |
| **L** | | Everything |
| Learning | | Experiment |
| Linking | | Empiricism |

## Intention

**Objectives:**
1. Understand the role of intent in providing guardrails.
2. Realize who is responsible for questioning the intent.
3. Harmonize intent, goals, and outcome-based focus.

The real benefit of working and thinking in a more A.G.I.L.E. way when your intention is to create something new or innovative is that we are able to get the feedback quickly, apply that feedback, see the results, and then iterate on the next most valuable piece of work.

As you can see, there is no need to live in an either-or world of A.G.I.L.E. versus a plan-driven deterministic way of thinking; it is all about figuring out what approach suits you best for the given intention. As we evaluate how to think about our products, we need to evaluate how well they are understood and determine whether we have invested all the effort we want in them. If not, is the product being disrupted, and are we doing the disrupting so others do not? Once we have made this choice, we can then optimize for efficiency. This probably applies to the majority of products under consideration in the world; however, when you have a product that does meet the criteria discussed, it would be wise to consider how you can begin thinking in a more A.G.I.L.E. way. The benefits will accrue to the organization, the knowledge worker, and the customers.

For many, agile is a new tool in the toolbox that will allow for the selection of the appropriate actions while the journey is underway without the need to make the decisions when uncertainty is the highest, which is at the beginning of the endeavor. Another common example of the benefits of A.G.I.L.E. thinking can be seen when we have a massive number of customers whom we cannot go to and individually ask their opinion for what they would want in a product. This makes the plan-driven, deterministic approach almost impossible to yield the benefits that this approach used to get. It is more likely we will be able to get the feedback we need only when we put something in their hands. This drives us to use empiricism to make small changes so that we do not over invest in the wrong things that the customers do not see as valuable.

Intention allows for something new to come from the empirical approach. It is the direction of our pursuit that matters most or, in other words, the outcomes we intend. The intention is articulated in the goals that the team creates for every increment. It is what we evaluate ourselves against in the end and encourages us to inspect and adapt our approach to get to the outcomes we seek.

Just as goals must be committed to by the group that is endeavoring to reach them, intention must also be well understood. If the product's intention is not communicated or not well understood, the team cannot commit to it. It is crucial to note when we should be using the empirical versus the plan-driven approach. If the task is straightforward and well understood, we should seek the use of plan- and process-driven approaches to deal with complicated operations. There is no need to invest in the expense and effort of trying to convince people that there is a need for the empirical method. There is still benefit to people working and thinking in a more A.G.I.L.E. way simply because it helps teams to become higher performing through communication and collaboration. Unfortunately, where we see organizations applying the A.G.I.L.E. way of thinking is with endeavors that are complicated but lack the uncertainty and complexity that demand the empirical approach to problem-solving.

**Reflection:**
1. How can we introduce people to the idea of intent?
2. Who gives the intent and who needs to understand the intent?
3. How do goals, intent, and outcomes play together?

| A | G | I |
|---|---|---|
| Accountability | Goal | Intention |
| Alignment | | Invitation |
| Application | | Innovation |
| Attitude | | Ideas |
| Attention | | Increment |
| Action | | Information |
| Absorb | | Impact |
| Agency | | **E** |
| **L** | | Everything |
| Learning | | Experiment |
| Linking | | Empiricism |

## Invitation

1. Understand that each organization is different and that the journey will be unique.
2. Acknowledge how the response to the invitation will determine the next best action.
3. Recognize that there will be situations that will require a more plan-driven approach.

Invitation is critical for moving individuals in a direction that will lead to operating in an A.G.I.L.E. way. This invitation will need to be supported and done with integrity, even when it cannot be fully understood. It will be very difficult to shift to what another organization did to get to the outcomes they achieved and apply that approach directly to your organization. There are too many variables that need to be analyzed to know which aspects to apply and which ones to disregard.

If we begin with an invitation to work and think in an A.G.I.L.E. way, we will have less analysis and more empiricism to guide us on our journey. By inviting someone in, we are able to hold the individual accountable for learning to think in this new way. Although some will learn the terminology and the mechanics of agile without beginning to think in an A.G.I.L.E. way, it will become evident, and they can be invited to continue to work in a plan-driven environment. There will still be people who are needed to operate within the plan-driven approach, and rightly so. This is not a silver bullet to solve all problems; it is a well-understood and well-analyzed way of approaching highly complex and highly uncertain problems. We will need people with a desire and propensity to have an organization that thinks in an A.G.I.L.E. way.

As people begin to grow, they will need to have integrity with one another. The way to success will rest on the ability for individuals to gain trust in one another. The command and control approach is based on adherence to direction. The empirical method will require individuals to make and keep agreements with one another based on invitation. There is no plan to point to when things go wrong; there is only the conversation and connections made within the team. These connections rest with whatever integrity each team member has with one another. If those connections are weak or not transparent, there will be little accountability to the goals that were committed to. If there is not a full-throated commitment to seek the goal, there will be low engagement.

With A.G.I.L.E., we are shifting the commitment from adherence to a plan or obeying a directive to engaging at the human level to seek the goals that have been mutually agreed upon to pursue. The short increments of value delivery are designed to allow for the experience to be fresh in everyone's mind when they come together and reflect on how to get better. If these interactions are not authentic, they will be of little value. If the group has not come together as a true team with a common long-lived purpose, the value of A.G.I.L.E. thinking cannot be realized.

A.G.I.L.E. thinking is different than traditional change initiatives because we are dealing with human interactions based on trust. If teams are allowed to avoid the tough work of building trust with one another, they will not reach their potential and will most likely not stay a team for very long. There is also the risk that as long as people are not identifying as a team, any friction will be seen as something to be managed by traditional managers. If this is done again and again, the team will not be required to self-solve the issues that will make them a better team for having gone through the experience.

Integrity also applies to the customer interaction. There will be disappointments and failure when we set goals that may or may not be attainable in the increment we set out in. Learning must take place for everyone who has not been working this way before. Those that have previously been exposed to this way of working, whether team member or customer, and have the agile mindset will still need to build trust with the individuals on the new team. There are no shortcuts to getting to trust; it must be built one interaction at a time.

**Reflection:**

1. What types of things might make an environment different from another?
2. What differences could be present within the same organization?
3. What impact will individual leaders have on the invitation process?

| A | G | I |
|---|---|---|
| Accountability | Goal | Intention |
| Alignment |  | Invitation |
| Application |  | Innovation |
| Attitude |  | Ideas |
| Attention |  | Increment |
| Action |  | Information |
| Absorb |  | Impact |
| Agency |  | **E** |
| **L** |  | Everything |
| Learning |  | Experiment |
| Linking |  | Empiricism |

## Innovation

**Objectives:**
1. Understand that creativity becomes available in certain environments.
2. Understand that there is a model in which creativity can scale.
3. Realize the supremacy of the team in this way of working.

One of the primary reasons agile is of great benefit is that it provides an opportunity for innovation by those involved in the process of creating value, whether this is in a product or capability that would otherwise be very difficult to create in a plan-driven manner.

If we take the same approach with people allocation that we have with the plan-driven approach in highly complex and highly uncertain environments, we will not yield the value to grow a highly competent team for solving the types of problems we are seeking to solve.

Creativity is the key to problem-solving in these environments, and we need to build teams that can solve problems creatively together.

We know that we will need to scale to be able to solve really large problems and will therefore need to scale what we seek: highly capable teams that can creatively solve problems.

This can be achieved by inviting people to become part of something that will interest them and allow them to work in a way that makes sense for them. If we can bring people together who have the skills needed and allow them to form as a team, we will be much more likely to get the outcomes we seek.

In order for an agile team to be able to form, it needs time to do so; not days but weeks and months. This is not to say we do not get results from the team for months. It means we begin to get better and better results as the team is able to work together, understand each other, and build trust in one another. This is something that can be observed to determine when it is working and when it is not.

Once the right team dynamics form, any change in the team makeup will necessitate a step back to the beginning of the trust journey of the team. It is counterintuitive that if you must change the team members, taking away is better than adding. The trust level will see some disturbance if there is someone removed from the team; however, it will create nowhere near the same level of disruption that would result from a member added to the team. This new understanding of team will frustrate the resource-driven optimization approach, where the only determination of who is assigned to work is their skill or experience. In this A.G.I.L.E. way of thinking, we are looking for the team to be the problem-solving engine and not the individuals that happen to be working in close proximity. Again, we are redefining how leaders work, and, fundamentally, their largest contribution to success will be the proper selection of individuals for the team and then the discipline the leaders will need to allow the team to figure the rest out among themselves. This does not mean the leader does not have a heavy and challenging workload to deal with; the leader is needed to remove any impediments to the A.G.I.L.E. way of working. Impediments surround the team because we are just now creating a team that is chartered to work in an A.G.I.L.E. way while everyone else is working in a plan-driven deterministic approach.

The fundamental shift in how we allow the team to stay together for extended periods in order to help them grow is at odds with many of the management constructs in place within corporations today. Many of the current constructs optimize for a properly selected plan-driven approach, which seeks to optimize resource allocation, just like an assembly line. When we are dealing with processes that have variance, we have a feedback mechanism in place. The requisite inspection points of this approach are fine for simple projects with clear outcomes, such as when we are making cars that have a specific set of outcome characteristics. If we continue to use the same leadership choices we have previously used, we will be at odds with the empirical approach to solving problems through experimentation.

Leaders need to find those who are willing to defend the experiments of the team while they learn and grow to the point of freely experimenting before true innovation begins to happen. One way leaders can support this process is through better and smaller problem definition. If we can better define the leader's and team's our problem solving roles by thinking differently about roles and accountability, it will yield clarity of the problem. As teams and leaders begin respecting their individual problem-solving roles, they begin to trust others to play their own part in the journey, as well. This begins to allow for people to focus their energy based on their role instead of functions. A simple example is to have someone define the what without defining the how, while another, most likely from the group, defines the how.

Functional focus is an impediment to A.G.I.L.E. way of thinking because there is not a common product-driven goal when people are aligning to the success of their function. Many discuss shifting to a product focus, which will break the functional bonds of individual team members. In the end, this hinders the potential of teams to be able to focus on a single goal. The idea of function is a throwback to the industrial age when our focus was to make the work more and more discrete so that we could get efficiencies. When we apply the A.G.I.L.E. way of thinking to the appropriate context, we can see why this put us in conflict with the focus of a common goal. In software, we are less constrained by the physical world, so there is less hard knowledge that needs to be understood.

When we bring people together, it is more for their ability to collaborate than it is for their functional expertise.

Thinking in an A.G.I.L.E. way also challenges this alignment to function versus product-based goals. Many are uncomfortable pitching in outside their function until they realize we need problem-solvers working on high-performing teams. Unless we can let go of the plan-driven approach when it comes to creating innovative products and services, we will not understand or enjoy the benefits of A.G.I.L.E.

A.G.I.L.E. thinking requires a higher level of dependency awareness and understanding of the causes of those dependencies. Dependencies are sometimes perceived as friction; friction is valuable and happens in nature, while dependencies are constructs of the organization to ensure control. We need to make sure we are working to remove dependencies for the high-performing team. Dependencies are an artifact of the plan-driven approach to getting work done and are constructed by discrete manufacturing techniques where we are able to become more and more discrete in the components of work to drive efficiency. When we are thinking in an A.G.I.L.E. way, we are seeking effective outcomes instead of seeking efficiency. Efficiency is a goal for largely repetitive work, whether that work be simple or complicated. We seek efficiency because we already have the outcome understood. When we seek to manage dependencies, we are not eliminating the organizational impediments team needs to have to reach the product goal. While the systems needs to support the work, much more attention needs to be paid to enabling the team to produce a working product.

Managing dependencies does not mean we are eliminating them forever, however that should be our goal now. If we are continually discussing the management of the same dependencies as we tend to do in plan-driven environments, we will not be moving toward working in an A.G.I.L.E. way. Most dependencies can be seen in very small experiments within A.G.I.L.E. It's how those dependencies are dealt with that will determine whether A.G.I.L.E. thinking is being embraced. Are the dependencies being eliminated or managed? Are they being dealt with by the team alone, or does the team get strong support from the leaders who are most likely the same leaders that created the dependencies? When we look for innovation, we see it in small nimble groups of people that are normally free of the large-scale dependency management systems that are the hallmark of traditional organizations. This is why innovation is lacking in many organizations. The innovation comes from wholistic, product-focused approaches to problem-solving. As soon as we allow dependencies to become what we manage instead of outcomes, we lose focus on product-focused goals. When dependencies are addressed by people in positions to eliminate them, amazing things begin to happen. Without that level of leadership, teams continue to struggle with the flow of work and momentum suffers.

Thinking in an A.G.I.L.E. way will invite a new way of communicating that is a lot less structured and status driven. As we begin to become more empirical in our approaches and as we embrace A.G.I.L.E., we will be operating in the present moment. There is little need to speak of the work that is being done prospectively. Most of the work that is best suited to the A.G.I.L.E. way of thinking is not deterministic; therefore, it is less useful to discuss what might happen. The idea of being specific in our projections and commitments to outcomes comes from the plan-driven approach to getting work done. As we have seen, that approach does not yield the outcomes we seek; however, we use all of the same mechanisms to predict the outcomes nonetheless. The communication and the conversations need to shift to the goals that are being sought at each level, and the most likely place for those goals to be out of alignment is in the middle of the organization, the space between the people actually doing the work and the executives setting strategic vision. The alignment conversation will be elevated by talented leaders who are able to describe what is being sought in the product goals that will align to the organization's higher-level goals while becoming an encourager of experimentation to the teams. This will take immense courage at the middle level of the organization, a level of courage that has not been required in the industrial age.

This courage is in contrast to what is often seen in the middle layer of organizations that are designed to ensure communication of status, which is not necessarily a courageous endeavor, especially when the middle is able to shield the higher and lower levels of the organization from one another. As soon as we begin to embrace the "come see attitude," we will see clarity and awareness and, hopefully, alignment through robust and transparent conversation. This conversation can accelerate A.G.I.L.E. thinking throughout large organizations.

Every level of the organization will need to focus on cascading the message while translating that message to a level that allows the teams and individuals to clearly understand the focus of their work. When that understanding is achieved, there is an environment where A.G.I.L.E. thinking takes off. The impact of meeting in the middle will be seen as we apply A.G.I.L.E. thinking to the conversation, and we will begin to have an impact on the effectiveness of the organization, again from the bottom up and from the top down. If the same plan-driven constructs are used to begin thinking in an A.G.I.L.E. way, we will not make a successful transition to A.G.I.L.E.

Innovation is not the goal of A.G.I.L.E.; it is the result. There is no innovation switch that gets flipped and it is not a process that can be designed.

> Innovation comes from standing in a different place that learning and experience has brought the team to and allowing the team to see new challenges, feel the sense of urgency, and set their intention in a new direction.

The intention will drive the goals they create by standing in that new place. It will allow the next increment to take place before the cycle begins again with the new awareness, whether the last increment was a success or not. Some will be successful in this transition, and some will not; however, when learning has taken place, the same challenge will be different in the next increment because learning has already taken place. We are undertaking creative endeavors with high complexity and high uncertainty, and just because we have attempted something once, it does not mean we have all the learning needed to get it right the next time. This is why A.G.I.L.E. thinking is so valuable once it is understood, embraced, and practiced. A.G.I.L.E. allows for the possibility of innovation.

**Reflection:**
1. What role does the leader play in the development of a team?
2. If a change is needed in the members of a high-performing team, what should it be?
3. Why does it take time for a team to become high performing?

| **A** | **G** | **I** |
|---|---|---|
| Accountability | Goal | Intention |
| Alignment | | Invitation |
| Application | | Innovation |
| Attitude | | Ideas |
| Attention | | Increment |
| Action | | Information |
| Absorb | | Impact |
| Agency | | **E** |
| **L** | | Everything |
| Learning | | Experiment |
| Linking | | Empiricism |

## Ideas

**Objectives:**
1. Understand that scaling is a delicate dance.
2. Realize the leader's role in psychological safety.
3. Determine where ideas come from within an organization.

A.G.I.L.E. thinking helps us improve how we experiment with new ideas. When we, as a group, have new ideas, are we able to capture them? Are we able to brainstorm in safety? People who have been working in a deterministic environment for years will struggle to feel safe to explore ideas or even to vocalize them. When we are critical of the ideas being expressed, there is little opportunity to build upon them and explore the possibilities. If we are putting our gut to use, we will most likely come out with an incomplete idea that needs the help of the team to become viable. If we are thinking in a plan-driven way, we will become biased toward figuring out how we would do such a thing instead of first figuring out whether the idea has merit to even go to the next step of coming up with an experiment to see how to get it done. These challenges are real when we begin to think in an A.G.I.L.E. way, and with experience, leaders can recognize and provide psychological safety and encouragement for this type of interaction to begin.

While the organization constructs will dictate the need to scale, scaling does not necessarily mean the value is being multiplied by the complex structures put in place. Dunbar's number states that we, as humans, can only maintain so many emotional connections. That number is estimated to be between 125 and 150. If we can leverage how our biology is set up to constrain our scaling ambitions, we can see enormous leverage and output toward our desired outcome. As you think about scaling, consider the number of human connections that will be in play while you are organizing to deliver value. Refrain from creating complex matrixed organizations that optimize for the efficiency of specialists, and begin to allow for a learning organization to emerge over time. To do this you will need to be purposeful in designing for high-performing teams, the majority of whose success is determined before they even come together. This can no longer be an exercise where organizational power brokers put names in boxes to maintain their functional control in the organization. The organizational design will need to focus on products and customer personas to ensure we always have a view for whom the product is being built.

Ideas are all around us. In innovative organizations, everyone is involved in the creation process because their future is not just left to those few who have a specific domain expertise. If that occurs, it is a recipe for more of the same, which is often characterized as incremental improvement instead of great new ideas that lead to innovation.

**Reflection:**
1. How, as a leader, do you support psychological safety?
2. How does Dunbar's number inform our approach to scaling?
3. Who is responsible for ideas in an innovative organization?

| **A** | **G** | **I** |
|---|---|---|
| Accountability | Goal | Intention |
| Alignment | | Invitation |
| Application | | Innovation |
| Attitude | | Ideas |
| Attention | | Increment |
| Action | | Information |
| Absorb | | Impact |
| Agency | | **E** |
| **L** | | Everything |
| Learning | | Experiment |
| Linking | | Empiricism |

## Increment

**Objectives:**

1. Understand that the increment is the primary tool for improvement.
2. Realize that the increment is a forcing mechanism for feedback.
3. Be aware that the increment is a two-edged sword on the journey to greater agility.

A.G.I.L.E. thinking will yield outsized benefits when used for the appropriate situations. The increment is one of the first ways we can determine whether we have an appropriate use case for this approach. If we can break down the work to get small batch sizes, there is a good chance we can use the increment to inspect and adapt our product and the way we are working together as a team. Once we have the cadence of this approach underway, we will be able to see how we progress and improve from increment to increment. Keep in mind that the situation will change from one increment to the next because we are working within the context of high uncertainty and high complexity.

As soon as we seek consistency from increment to increment, we have deluded ourselves into thinking we are deterministic and have become plan-driven again.

The increment is useful to help us inspect and adapt at getting better over time. *What are we trying to get better at?* We want to get better at working together as a team, at setting goals, and at learning from failure.

While the increment may look like a small plan-driven increment, it is an arbitrary construct. The increment is a manufactured deterministic break used to allow for feedback to be received, digested, and incorporated into what will be done next. If this cycle is not occurring, there is little benefit to be gained by stopping, which is what is often suggested when there is not a robust feedback cycle from the appropriate people to provide input to the team. This feedback is desperately needed to course correct and deliver higher value.

The increment is the bridge between the plan-driven world and the empirical world of A.G.I.L.E.

When used in the appropriate way, it can be something of a handhold for people making the transition. The caution here is that if the input and outputs are not being evaluated on an empirical level by the right people, the pendulum may well swing quickly back to the plan-driven approach.

**Reflection:**
  1. Why is the increment so powerful?
  2. Why is the increment so dangerous?
  3. What determines the success of the incremental approach?

| **A** | **G** | **I** |
|---|---|---|
| Accountability | Goal | Intention |
| Alignment | | Invitation |
| Application | | Innovation |
| Attitude | | Ideas |
| Attention | | Increment |
| Action | | Information |
| Absorb | | Impact |
| Agency | | **E** |
| **L** | | Everything |
| Learning | | Experiment |
| Linking | | Empiricism |

## Information

**Objectives:**
1. Demonstrate the importance of thinking with the information at hand.
2. Recognize the time to make decisions is different in this way of working.
3. Determine the right time to make decisions in this model.

With A.G.I.L.E., information becomes more dynamic and less polished. The idea is that we need directional indicators that help us work. When we get bogged down in the information, we are taking focus away from the outcomes and are falling back into the plan-driven approach of monitoring the progress instead of inspecting the product. As we saw with the increment, information will be critical to be able to make intelligent decisions and pivot quickly. If that information is not forthcoming at the end of every cycle from the appropriate individuals, there will be little value in the pursuit of improving. The experience will fade, and context will be lost quickly.

Unlike the plan-driven approach, where most of the information is used for monitoring, the majority of information within the A.G.I.L.E. way of thinking is used to make intelligent decisions and act.

The increment, which incorporates current information, allows for action to be taken much more often than when we are using a plan-driven approach. The plan in the empirical approach is for very short cycles that allow for a new plan about every 2 weeks at the larger scale and every day on the smaller scale.

The ability to respond to change and the willingness to do so is also important. The quality of the information is one of the factors that allow the team to pivot in a new direction when necessary. If we are unable to gain feedback from the proper people, the pivot direction will be less certain, and when the pivot does occur, there is less clarity on how the new information should be interpreted. This requires rawer visceral data to be used and interpreted by those that have the ability to decide or take an action. If you are not in one of those groups, you should be in a role of support and not of directing. This is another good way to understand whether A.G.I.L.E. thinking is being embraced. The organizational construct of command and control are released, and those within that construct become support for the people making the bets and doing the work.

A.G.I.L.E. thinking, or any thinking for that matter, will help us get better. The organizational intelligence of where to go next or what to do next will be critical for keeping the momentum going in the right direction. We need to improve our understanding of the intelligence we have and what the focus needs to be. We need to accelerate the use of our intelligence when working in an A.G.I.L.E. way because we are no longer supported by a plan that lays out in detail the next 18 to 24 months. We are now held to a model that requires everyone to make decisions at the last responsible moment. This applies to the high-level managers all the way down to the individual on the team deciding how a product will be created. If any one person is given more time than is absolutely needed, momentum will begin to slow and intelligence cannot be applied with the focus required to create within an increment. When we do not create some working product within an increment, we need to question which construct we are operating within: the plan-driven or emperical approach.

**Reflection:**
1. How will you shift the time when you make decisions?
2. How will you make the increment your companion?
3. What does the last responsible moment look like to you when you have imperfect information?

| **A** | **G** | **I** |
|---|---|---|
| Accountability | Goal | Intention |
| Alignment | | Invitation |
| Application | | Innovation |
| Attitude | | Ideas |
| Attention | | Increment |
| Action | | Information |
| Absorb | | Impact |
| Agency | | **E** |
| **L** | | Everything |
| Learning | | Experiment |
| Linking | | Empiricism |

## Impact

**Objectives:**

1. Realize the importance of planning in the moment with what we know.
2. Practice planning with the realization we need to be focused on impact as we go.
3. Practice planning around shared goals without the decomposition of the goal.

Working in an A.G.I.L.E. way will invite acceptance of the current reality. It is common when we work in a plan-driven environment that we are more likely to be looking forward or backward, instead of working in the moment. The moment is when we can have an impact. We can imagine how things could, should, or would happen; however, we have no direct impact on a future moment. The future is a blank sheet. We do need to know what we are going after in the future, and we do this by creating a backlog and prioritizing the backlog in a way that value comes into existence. This is where a future back view is useful to help guide the activities of the team. This is often when the important conversations of what to do next is richly engaged in. Without such conversation, there is little hope for alignment around shared goals. Without shared goals, which are unlikely in traditional organizations owing to the historical organizational constructs, we will lack the focus that is required by having very tight timeboxes to deliver value.

I am not saying that planning is bad or that it should not be done; however, we need to be aware that when we plan we are always constraining ourselves to solve a problem we do not understand. If we are to solve the problem, we will need to gain understanding through learning.

In the empirical approach to generating desirable outcomes, we must interrogate reality one step at a time so we can learn what to do next.

The "what to do next" is the value of thinking in an A.G.I.L.E. way. It is not the plan with the well-defined deterministic milestones, budgets, and deliverables that will yield the desired outcomes in highly complex, highly uncertain situations. It is the learning that will be gained by thinking in an A.G.I.L.E. way. Learning, however, is different than training or terminology, so it will need to be observed by people who have the experience and understanding to recognize A.G.I.L.E. thinking.

Once awareness of this new way of thinking comes to light with enough people from within the group, we can begin to experiment with what it means to the group and to the larger organization. When the larger group does not embrace this learning process, we see most of these initiatives become compromised and lose the value that this new way of thinking enables. The reality is that it is not the way of thinking that is flawed; it is the organization's response to the new way of thinking that will eliminate any hope of it taking hold at the scale the organization will need for the outsized benefits to be realized. The awareness that there is a higher likelihood of failure than success will steel the champions for the work ahead of them. In this case, we are using champions because it is not the traditional leaders that are going to be doing the work day in and day out to help people move toward the A.G.I.L.E. way of thinking; it is the people that have, for whatever reason, been exposed to this new approach, have gained some learning, and have begun to leave behind the plan-driven, deterministic approach and embraced the A.G.I.L.E. way of thinking.

**Reflection:**
1. How will planning need to change to be effective?
2. Who will need to be involved in planning for it to be effective?
3. How often will plans need to change if we are planning effectively in an A.G.I.L.E. way?

| A | G | I |
|---|---|---|
| Accountability | Goal | Intention |
| Alignment | | Invitation |
| Application | | Innovation |
| Attitude | | Ideas |
| Attention | | Increment |
| Action | | Information |
| Absorb | | Impact |
| Agency | | **E** |
| **L** | | Everything |
| Learning | | Experiment |
| Linking | | Empiricism |

## Learning

**Objectives:**

1. Demonstrate the value proposition of thinking in an A.G.I.L.E. way.
2. Understand the value of thinking in a deterministic way.
3. Determine the new way of leading.

As we have explored the different aspects of thinking in an A.G.I.L.E. way, we have described indicators that let us know whether we are holding on to an inappropriate way of thinking or embracing A.G.I.L.E. The impact of thinking in an A.G.I.L.E. way is evident at every encounter as we begin to understand the plan-driven approach and its usefulness compared with A.G.I.L.E. There are many approaches to injecting more agility into an organization; however, there are very few ways to shift the thinking of an individual, a team, and a larger organization. It's important that we recognize that we have had many changes during the industrial age; however, most of them, if not all, have furthered the plan-driven approach. Thinking in an A.G.I.L.E. way is counter to a long line of approaches and techniques that have served us well when doing deterministic work, and those approaches should be practiced and preserved when doing that same type of work. They should not, however, be confused with thinking in an A.G.I.L.E. way. As long as we can focus on the behavior being displayed, we will be able to discern whether we are moving toward the positive impact of A.G.I.L.E. or resisting it by main-taining the well-understood plan-driven, deterministic approaches.

Learning is of primary importance, and we will need to learn to lead differently if we are to lead in an A.G.I.L.E. way. There is little room in this new highly complex, highly uncertain environment for the tradi-tional plan-driven approach to get desired outcomes. We need to accel-erate our learning by allowing more experimentation and ensuring the iterations are much shorter.

When we make big bets in the plan-driven approach, we have well-defined plans that have often been executed many times by individuals with the experience in the domain and plans themselves. By contrast, we do not have much in the way of certainty in A.G.I.L.E., so we need to account for that in our approach to achieving the desired outcomes.

> We need to learn:
> 1. How to think differently
> 2. How to lead differently
> 3. A new set of tools and skills

Things can go terribly wrong when we confuse the environment we are operating in. This is what is happening when people are attempt-ing to lead in a highly uncertain environment using outdated leadership approaches or, even worse, using management approaches when attempt-ing to lead people.

Once we understand the steps to leading in an uncertain environ-ment, we free ourselves from heavyweight planning and begin to create deterministic pauses to do the inspecting and adapting that experimenta-tion demands. The shift is conceptually not hard to understand; we all did experiments in high school, we have all tried to learn something new, and we have all tried a new route to work or navigated in a new city. Why is it so difficult for us to realize this in the new digital technology-driven disruption our organizations are experiencing today? How many times have we heard "it takes what it takes" when it comes to doing some-thing that cannot be done with a well-worn plan or procedure? Does that mean we do not learn by trying, or are we so used to operating in a low change environment, or one we have defined as such, when in reality we have frozen the variables so we can be right instead of being successful?

The external environment has overwhelmed our defenses against change, and now we must respond. Responsible leadership is needed to move the organization in a dynamic way to enable learning by doing and failing. If we are able to make smaller and smaller bets and get feedback from those bets, we can move more quickly toward the outcomes we seek. The outcomes are the results of the outputs we produce from all of the thousands of experiments we will need to make to be able to achieve the desired outcomes.

In this new way of leading, we will need a different measurement approach since the current plan-driven approach measures against a plan instead of getting closer to the outcomes we seek. We see this clearly in the massive divide between information technology and business in many traditional plan-driven organizations that are now seeking to innovate, or just keep up with the innovation that others are doing within their industries.

Which one of Edison's experiments was not needed? He did not know, so how can we, in an empirical way, know which of the approaches or experiments will yield the results we seek? We have come to the point that we need to embrace the uncertainty of business and allow the empirical approach to impact parts of the organization that need to be innovated. There is certainly no need for everything in an organization to be run in an A.G.I.L.E. way; that would produce waste. If there is no need or desire for the process or product to change, we should use traditional approaches to eliminate waste.

It does not mean we should not or cannot lead people to get the best from them for the organization, and have a much more robust process-driven approach to the operation.

The leaders of this new approach to working in domains with high uncertainty and high variability will need a new language to be able to find support for the experimentation needed to get to outcomes. This does not mean that what is being tried cannot be done; most of what we see today are organizations trying to move incrementally in a direction that others have already taken. Why is it so hard for some of us to follow what others have demonstrated can be done? It is not something that will take enormous talent or skills developed over years of training and study, or is it? If we manage one way today and want to lead a different way tomorrow, what will need to be different in order to make that possible? We will need to embrace an empirical approach to problem-solving when the problem calls for it. We will also need the skills to identify individuals who have that ability, just as we identified people in the past who were well suited to the hierarchical approach to managing complicated environments. Leaders will need to understand the constructs in which one approach is likely to work well and those in which a different approach is required.

The first step in learning to lead in this new way is to understand that there is more than one way to lead and that, given where most of the desired change is focused, we need to focus heavily on the empirical learning model. The reasons for the extra focus are the following:

1. It is new to many of the leaders and managers within the organization.
2. This approach is drastically different from how people were managed in the past.
3. This approach takes a high trust environment and a level of vulnerability that is not seen in many corporate cultures.

It is unfortunate that we have lost the desire to seek excellence in many organizations because we try to demonstrate compliance with a plan. When we are driven by a plan that has a low probability of being accurate because of when it was conceived and use it for an endeavor that is highly uncertain and highly complex, we often lose sight of the goal we have in mind and focus on adherence to the plan. If the goal is important, we should focus on the outcomes we are seeking and strive to meet those as quickly as possible, or at least gain evidence that we are moving in a good direction.

Ben Franklin started each day with the same question and ended it with a different question: "What good shall I do today?" and "What good did I do today?" A day is a very short iteration, and we can achieve really big outcomes by ourselves; however, there is a way to lead that will invite the participation of many toward a goal that can be achieved incrementally and can be inspected and adapted through small increments.

One of the obvious differences in many organizations that seek to begin working in a more A.G.I.L.E. way is the environmental considerations they are making by moving away from the high-walled cubicle farms. While this change is sometimes very effective when done well and when the organization takes into consideration how people who are working with high complexity and high uncertainty work best, this is not a "one size fits all" approach. One of the best ways to begin to demonstrate trust in the people that are solving these challenges is to allow them to decide how they can best organize to achieve the goals.

As potentially helpful as the physical environment can be, the mental constructs become much more critical. If we compare this with a properly applied plan-driven approach, we see fundamental differences in regard to how people are applied to get the work accomplished. In a plan-driven approach, we seek to optimize the sequencing and expertise of individuals to ensure as little waste as possible. When doing complicated processes, we have found that this is the best approach. While there is a need for continued improvement, we seek to inspect the output of the process and respond to change when we get variance outside of the acceptable limits. This approach falls short when we are working with high uncertainty and complexity. We literally do not know what good looks like in most cases.

**Reflection:**
1. How can we talk about experimentation in a way that it does not invite an accusation of waste?
2. What can leaders do to support the impact of experimentation?
3. How do you describe the difference of impact with the plan-driven approach versus the A.G.I.L.E. way of working?

| A | G | I |
|---|---|---|
| Accountability | Goal | Intention |
| Alignment | | Invitation |
| Application | | Innovation |
| Attitude | | Ideas |
| Attention | | Increment |
| Action | | Information |
| Absorb | | Impact |
| Agency | | **E** |
| **L** | | Everything |
| Learning | | Experiment |
| Linking | | Empiricism |

## Linking

**Objectives:**
1. Understand that the source of inputs changes with uncertainty.
2. Determine how to use feedback as input.
3. Realize that risk is managed differently in this new way of working.

Shifting the inputs we seek is critical to better the outputs we desire. The alignment of the outputs in the direction of the outcomes we go after will need to improve. Oftentimes, we seek input from people who are not doing the work or who are not talking to the customer. The idea that the people doing the work know more about the work than those that are managing the people doing the work is still a foreign concept in many large, well-established organizations. It works well to have people in positions separated from both the work and the customer driving the work and the expected outcomes when we are in a highly predictable endeavor with little variability within the output and where there is little flexibility of the customer. However, we are increasingly seeing that we need to operate in the space of high uncertainty and high complexity, and this will mean we have a need for different and more varied input sources.

A.G.I.L.E. will drive the need for more linking of these historically disconnected concepts in the forms of feedback. Analysis will not be of as much value as it has been in the past owing to the uncertainty of the outcomes we seek.

There is inherently higher risk when operating in an A.G.I.L.E. way; however, that does not mean it cannot be effectively managed. The linking of individuals is the key to managing the inherent risk within A.G.I.L.E.

We invest much less when operating in an A.G.I.L.E. way and can pivot quickly based on linking the feedback we receive. This shorter interaction and risk mitigation approach works only if we are getting true feedback from someone who is using the product and is paying or willing to pay for it. If we get feedback from people who are not of these groups, it may not link to the intentions we seek and will need to be discounted.

The shift in the type of outcomes that organizations are going after has occurred without the requisite shift in how those outcomes are being sought. The outcomes we seek are tied to the input we get and separated by the outputs of the team that is delivering against the team's short-term goals. It is up to the customer to link the feedback to the next cycle so it can begin again. If there is no energy or involvement from the customer, only the lower-level benefits of working and thinking in an A.G.I.L.E. way, such as collaboration and communication, will be realized; however, that may not be worth the investment and energy it takes to move an entire organization toward thinking in an A.G.I.L.E. way.

INPUTS generate OUTPUTS not necessarily OUTCOMES

There is no guarantee that outputs will produce the outcomes we seek. That is why we need to build strong linkages between many of these concepts.

**Reflection:**
1. How do you determine the use cases for this approach?
2. What experiments could be run to determine how to strengthen the linkages?
3. How do you identify a feedback loop?

| A | G | I |
|---|---|---|
| Accountability | Goal | Intention |
| Alignment | | Invitation |
| Application | | Innovation |
| Attitude | | Ideas |
| Attention | | Increment |
| Action | | Information |
| Absorb | | Impact |
| Agency | | **E** |
| **L** | | Everything |
| Learning | | Experiment |
| Linking | | Empiricism |

# Everything

**Objectives:**
1. Determine why everything will likely change.
2. Understand the sequence of change in your particular context.
3. Embrace the idea of changing everything over time.

In order to work in an A.G.I.L.E. way, everything will need to be looked at in a new light. We cannot make small, safe changes and expect the environment to change to yield something that has been very difficult to achieve. The culture of an organization and the behaviors of that culture are ingrained when the culture is created. It will take enormous effort and focus to produce differences in the behavior first, and then as time and the expanding influence of the behaviors begin to take hold, significant benefits will begin to be realized. The leaders must be focused on this as a critical initiative, or else there will be little likelihood of real results. This cannot be just one more item on the to-do list; if it is to be, it must be something that a leader is willing to dedicate much of their time to in order to see real results in the absorption of this A.G.I.L.E. way of thinking. Many leaders will need to make the same shift we ask team leaders to make and to let go of the how and focus on the what.

The reasons for wanting to work in a more A.G.I.L.E. way are compelling, but like most things in our environment today, we will likely try and apply a plan-driven approach to getting to an A.G.I.L.E. way of thinking. That will expose the effort to all of the traps of going after something in a plan-driven fashion, which we do not know how to navigate. Unless you can go to the "factory floor" and hear and see the change, you are most likely leading a transformation by status report. In most cases, the change you can see with any earnest effort will be informative and even useful; however, the potential outsized gains will not materialize unless everything is challenged over time with willing participants.

**Reflection:**
1. Is your organization ready for such a change?
2. What experiments could you run to find out?
3. Where might you run these experiments first?

| A | G | I |
|---|---|---|
| Accountability | Goal | Intention |
| Alignment | | Invitation |
| Application | | Innovation |
| Attitude | | Ideas |
| Attention | | Increment |
| Action | | Information |
| Absorb | | Impact |
| Agency | | **E** |
| **L** | | Everything |
| Learning | | Experiment |
| Linking | | Empiricism |

# Experiment

**Objectives:**

1. Determine when experiments are appropriate.
2. Understand how to design good experiments.
3. Determine what you are trying to prove or disprove in the experiment.

In order to benefit from thinking in an A.G.I.L.E. way to any extent, we must constantly be getting feedback. The way we get feedback is to experiment. We need to find ways to sense every aspect of what we are trying to improve. If we are not trying to improve on a macro level, then we will be improving on a micro level. Thinking in an A.G.I.L.E. way helps us to improve on the micro level as we do not have the information to improve at the macro level yet. When we are trying to solve large problems with high uncertainty and high complexity, we may need to pivot significantly from where we are starting. This is an opportunity to experiment, sense, and respond very quickly. If we can design our experiments in a way where they will give us quick feedback, we will be more efficient in our efforts. We will be able to pivot quickly without remorse as we learn what is working for us and what is not. This is where awareness is critical; if we are not operating in the present, we will look back and see sunk cost and other hindrances to pivoting quickly. If we are stuck in the deterministic plan-driven approach, we will struggle with the idea of deviating from the plan to respond to the feedback we are receiving from the experiment just undertaken.

We must leave the idea of thinking of a failed experiment as a bad thing; this is the key to allowing us to develop our A.G.I.L.E. way of thinking. If there is no tolerance for speaking of failure, we can think of it as learning quickly. With a fixed mindset, we have developed an intense aversion to anything that appears to look like failure. This comes from early in our deterministic journey as we learn we are either right (a good feeling) or wrong (a bad feeling). This puts us in a box where experimentation is not welcome because we have an opportunity to be wrong. When we are wrong, we are opening ourselves to be judged, and in an environment that has not begun to think in an A.G.I.L.E. way, there is no allowance for the creative process that comes to us through experimentation.

In an environment that allows and encourages experimentation, the opposite becomes true over time, and the experimentation process is celebrated. While outcomes become more and more important, experimentation is how we get to the outcomes. Without embracing experimentation, we will only be able to incrementally improve what we have done or have seen others do and will not be able to create the changes we seek in a fast-paced changing world.

In our digital age, the ability to change is much more accessible to an increasing number of individuals and organizations. When we realize that there are now lower barriers to entry in many environments, organizations that did not need to concern themselves with the disruptions that others have seen are now under assault, even if it is only on the digital plane. The organizations that have previously been immune to competitive assault realize they need new tools to cope. A.G.I.L.E. thinking and the tools of experimentation allow creativity to take hold at an organizational level and become the engine of innovation.

Experimenting is the lifeblood of creativity and has been withheld from all but the most austere places within corporations; it was relegated to the R&D laboratories or other places outside of the mainstream of corporate life. We have now come to the digital age when all organizations are technology-based companies and the foundation is digital technology. Certainly, we have many systems within corporations that are outside of this realm; however, the vast majority of areas within the organization that need this level of leadership have something to do with technology.

Technology has driven massive disruptions in many areas where organizations thought they were immune to mass digitization. Think about groceries and books as two classic examples. Existing organizations are still solving the problems with a traditional plan-driven approach by bringing in someone who saw or even led the journey in another environment. That does not necessarily solve the problem within the organization that this leader is being introduced to. It is primarily the culture, the behaviors, and unspoken rules that are common knowledge within an organization that need to change. It will be very difficult for a new leader in an organization to lead the effort without support. It is often suggested that the support needs to come from the top of the organization. The approach advocated here is different; even if we get approval to lead a move in becoming more agile, it will be in situations that the leaders of the organization have not been exposed to. In large, well-established organizations, there most likely won't be anyone those leaders will trust to help them let go of so many of the constructs they have used in the past to achieve success. So where does the support come from for a new leader who may be well prepared to lead an effort to move in an agile direction? It must, by necessity, go back to the individuals who are invited to participate, and they must be willing to be led.

Oftentimes, the description of what is being sought after with A.G.I.L.E. thinking is described as a transformation. But a transformation from what to what? There are many dimensions that the transformation must occur in; however, none is more important than the level of leadership. One of the first things leaders need to do to make this transformation possible is to understand that their new roles in a highly complex and uncertain endeavor will take time, even for the willing. If we think someone from the outside can come in and do this to the organization, we will certainly miss the opportunity to lead in an A.G.I.L.E. way.

To begin this journey, we will need to do several things as a leader:

1. Understand the new highly complex and uncertain environment we operate in.
2. Embrace the idea of experimentation.
3. Embrace learning through failure.

**Reflection:**
1. How could you bring more experimentation into your life?
2. How could you bring more experimentation into your work?
3. What are some of the barriers to experimentation?

| A | G | I |
|---|---|---|
| Accountability | Goal | Intention |
| Alignment | | Invitation |
| Application | | Innovation |
| Attitude | | Ideas |
| Attention | | Increment |
| Action | | Information |
| Absorb | | Impact |
| Agency | | **E** |
| **L** | | Everything |
| Learning | | Experiment |
| Linking | | Empiricism |

## Empiricism

**Objectives:**

1. Understand how empiricism and planning complement each other.
2. Reconnect with empiricism through life experiences.
3. Determine where empiricism is needed within your context.

We have referenced empiricism throughout this book and contrasted it with the traditional plan-driven approach to getting work done. While the plan-driven approach is appropriate in many situations, it is not the best approach when dealing with highly uncertain and highly complex problems. We use the two dimensions of high uncertainty and high complexity together to drive home the idea that a different way of engaging in these situations is critical to success.

We have used the empirical approach to solve problems and achieve goals throughout our lives. The way we learned to walk was empirical, as was the way we learned to ride a bicycle. This approach is all around us when we are interacting in the physical world, so why is it so foreign to us now that we are operating in large organizations? The answer, which was suggested earlier, is that we are able to abstract ourselves from the physical world in many of the endeavors we undertake in large enterprises, especially within the digital context. As soon as we do this, we are able to fool ourselves into thinking the plan is reality. When we understand intuitively that the map is not the physical terrain, we are not so sure about the flawed nature of plans.

> We think that we can have a high level of certainty when we first begin our journey to create something we have not created before, with people we have not built a relationship of trust with, for people we do not know.

This is where the concept of empiricism comes to the rescue of so many and is beginning to be understood by larger and larger organizations that are coming out of the age of the plan-driven approach. This is not an easy journey for those that have been successful in the plan-driven approach to achieving results, and there may not have been a need for this new way of achieving work if it had not been for the emergence of software and the ability to abstract away the realities of the physical world. However, this is where we find ourselves, and we need empiricism to help us navigate the world of "if we can conceive of it, we can create it," even when we do not know if it is valuable or desirable and if it will draw customers to us and help us keep them engaged with us.

All of the various techniques that we have pointed to are written about in much detail in this series (see preface) and will be of value to you as you begin to think in an A.G.I.L.E. way. Without the right approach, those techniques will still be of some value as I have suggested elsewhere; however, the enormous potential of being agile will still elude you without the ability to think in an A.G.I.L.E. way. The empirical approach to problem-solving is the foundation for that thinking. It is not that we need to learn the empirical approach; it is more likely we need to remember it. We have all used it in our experiences interacting with the physical world and have left it by the wayside as we were able to abstract ourselves from needing to interact with the physical world for our work in large organizations.

**Reflection:**
1. How can you reconnect with the physical world to remember empiricism?
2. How can empiricism and planning live together in harmony?
3. How would you explain empiricism to a stranger?

# Conclusion

All change is difficult; however, in my four decades of challenging the status quo in the technology space, I have seen many transformations of how teams work and how effective and efficient they can be once we unleash the creativity and drive of the individual in a team setting. I firmly endorse the A.G.I.L.E. way of thinking and understand the tough work that will be required of the participants on this journey. Once we see small improvements, the momentum of change will allow us to overcome the inertia so prevalent in large enterprises. The possibilities are endless...

# About the Author

For over 30 years, Frank has led, participated in, and managed software projects and programs around the world for clients such as Wacom, Mylan Pharmaceutical, U.S. Army, U.S. Navy, U.S. Air Force, NASA, Computer Associates (CA), Computer Sciences Corporation (CSC), Verizon (GTE), Luxottica, The Christ Hospital, and ThyssenKrupp. He has worked across many different industries, including oil and gas, defense, software, government, CPGs (Consumer Packed Goods), industrial, healthcare, construction, manufacturing, and pharmaceuticals.

Today, Frank focuses on using agile principles to help empower and transform organizations. He understands the underlying lean and agile principles and the traditional software development life cycle, including their benefits and shortcomings. His breadth and depth of understanding cover information across the many spaces that agile touches.

Throughout Frank's software career he has experimented with extreme programing, pair programing, and other techniques to accelerate the effectiveness of teams. Frank started his career in the United States Navy while serving on nuclear-powered submarines. He spent 11 years in the Navy and was part of the crew that built the USS Atlanta (SSN 712). He led software projects as an architect, development lead, requirements lead, design lead, test lead, as well as program and project roles. He has spent the last 20 years focused primarily on software projects in various roles as Scrum Master, program and project manager, and delivery manager.

Frank is committed to the human interaction side of projects, particularly how leadership plays a key role in success and failure. He is pragmatic and realizes that any framework/solution is merely guidance based on the circumstances and is convinced that, in the end, people make the difference. He has been a student of the agile software movement and has introduced agile to different types and sizes of organizations.

Frank holds a Bachelor of Science in Computer Information Systems (BSCIS) and has done graduate work in software engineering. He is a SAFe program consultant, project management professional (PMP), certified Scrum Master (CSM), and a certified computer professional (CCP). He is a certified speaker, trainer, and coach with the John Maxwell Team. Frank is the president of Forte Leadership Technology, LLC.

# Index

# OTHER TITLES IN OUR PORTFOLIO AND PROJECT MANAGEMENT COLLECTION

Timothy Kloppenborg, *Editor*

- *Discoveries Through Personal Agility* by Raji Sivaraman and Michal Raczka
- *Project Communications: A Critical Factor for Project Success* by Connie Plowman and Jill Diffendal
- *Quantitative Tools of Project Management* by David L. Olson
- *The People Project Triangle: Balancing Delivery, Business-as-Usual, and People's Welfare* by Stuart Copeland and Andy Coaton
- *How to Fail at Change Management: A Manager's Guide to the Pitfalls of Managing Change* by James Marion and John Lewis
- *Core Concepts of Project Management* by David L. Olson
- *Projects, Programs, and Portfolios in Strategic Organizational Transformation* by James Jiang and Gary Klein
- *Capital Project Management, Volume III: Evolutionary Forces* by Robert N. McGrath
- *Capital Project Management, Volume II: Capital Project Finance* by Robert N. McGrath
- *Capital Project Management, Volume I: Capital Project Strategy* by Robert N. McGrath
- *Executing Global Projects: A Practical Guide to Applying the PMBOK Framework in the Global Environment* by James Marion and Tracey Richardson
- *Project Communication from Start to Finish: The Dynamics of Organizational Success* by Geraldine E. Hynes
- *The Lost Art of Planning Projects* by Louise Worsley and Christopher Worsley
- *Project Portfolio Management, Second Edition: A Model for Improved Decision Making* by Clive N. Enoch
- *Adaptive Project Planning* by Louise Worsley and Christopher Worsley
- *Passion, Persistence, and Patience: Key Skills for Achieving Project Success* by Alfonso Bucero
- *Leveraging Business Analysis for Project Success, Second Edition* by Vicki James
- *Project Management Essentials, Second Edition* by Kathryn N. Wells and Timothy J. Kloppenborg
- *Agile Working and the Digital Workspace: Best Practices for Designing and Implementing Productivity* by John Eary

## Concise and Applied Business Books

The Collection listed above is one of 30 business subject collections that Business Expert Press has grown to make BEP a premiere publisher of print and digital books. Our concise and applied books are for...

- Professionals and Practitioners
- Faculty who adopt our books for courses
- Librarians who know that BEP's Digital Libraries are a unique way to offer students ebooks to download, not restricted with any digital rights management
- Executive Training Course Leaders
- Business Seminar Organizers

**Business Expert Press** books are for anyone who needs to dig deeper on business ideas, goals, and solutions to everyday problems. Whether one print book, one ebook, or buying a digital library of 110 ebooks, we remain the affordable and smart way to be business smart. For more information, please visit **www.businessexpertpress.com**, or contact **sales@businessexpertpress.com**.

www.ingramcontent.com/pod-product-compliance
Lightning Source LLC
Chambersburg PA
CBHW052109230326
41599CB00054B/5272